THOMAS JEFFERSON
and the American Ideal

Thomas Jefferson

HENRY STEELE COMMAGER'S
AMERICANS

THOMAS JEFFERSON
and the American Ideal

BY RUSSELL SHORTO

Illustrations by Gary Gianni

Barron's Educational Series, Inc.

First edition published 1987
by Barron's Educational Series, Inc.

All inquiries should be addressed to:
Barron's Educational Series, Inc.
250 Wireless Blvd.
Hauppauge, NY 11788

Library of Congress Catalog Card No. 87-19454

International Standard Book No. 0-8120-3918-1

Library of Congress Cataloging-in-Publication Data

Shorto, Russell.
Thomas Jefferson and the American ideal.

(Henry Steele Commager's Americans)
Includes index.
Summary: Traces the life and achievements of the
Virginian who wrote the Declaration of Independence and
served as the third president of the United States.
1. Jefferson, Thomas, 1743-1826 — Juvenile literature.
2. Presidents — United States — Biography — Juvenile
literature. [1. Jefferson, Thomas, 1743-1826.
2. Presidents] I. Gianni, Gary, ill. II. Title.
III. Series.
E332.79.S56   1987   973.4'6'0924   [B]   [92]   87-19454
ISBN 0-8120-3918-1

Printed in the United States of America

456   9693   987

CONTENTS

Mr. Jefferson—no one ever called him "Tom"—was better at everything than anyone else. Though one of the youngest members of the 1776 Continental Congress, the others took for granted that he was the man to write a Declaration of Independence, and they were right. Thereafter, he was the man to be governor of Virginia; the one to work out plans for the creation of new states in the West, for public education and for the separation of church and state. Later, he was the man sent to join Benjamin Franklin in trying to win support for the American cause, and the one to write the Treaty of Peace with Britain. When Washington became president, he turned to Mr. Jefferson to be his secretary of state. After that he served as vice president under John Adams, and then became president himself for two terms. During all these years he continued to manage thirteen plantations—as farms were called in the South. He was easily the most skillful farmer in the country, always trying out new crops: he introduced rice to the southern states and different kinds of grapes, and brought over hundreds of olive trees. He was an inventor, too, whose plow won fame not only in America but in France and England. A lawyer as well, he had been thrown out of court early in his career because he argued that slavery was against the Laws of God and should be abolished. Although he owned slaves himself, he never changed that opinion and fought against slavery wherever he could throughout his life. It would be Mr. Jefferson who was responsible for the provision outlawing slavery in the new territories north of the Ohio River. A scholar who collected the largest library in America, he founded the Library of Congress to which he gave much of his own library. And finally, he was an architect who designed the capitol of his state and "his" University of Virginia. We can say "his" because he created it, appointed all the professors, drew up the curriculum, landscaped all the grounds, and chose the books for the library—as well as designing every building, every door, window, and fireplace. In all history there is no other institution so completely the creation of one man, and it was, and remains, the most beautiful marriage of buildings and grounds in America. As president, he acquired the Louisiana Purchase for the new nation—an area which included everything from the Mississippi River to the Rocky Mountains—and all for a mere fifteen million dollars. Then he sent out Lewis and Clark to explore this vast new region and lands beyond. They went all the way to the Pacific Ocean, confident, no doubt, as was Jefferson, that soon the United States would extend across the continent. He remained as busy in retirement as he had been in the White House, for it was then that he built his university. The end came in 1826 when both he and John Adams, another of the Founding Fathers who had been his friend much of his life, managed somehow to die on the same day, July 4th—the fiftieth anniversary of the Declaration of Independence.

Henry Steele Commager
Amherst, Massachusetts

CHAPTER ONE

A Job to Do

On the afternoon of June 7, 1776, bright summer sunlight streamed in through the windows of the Philadelphia State House. The delegates of the Second Congress of the American Colonies had just voted to declare America free of England's rule.

When the congressional session adjourned, the excited delegates rushed out to spread the startling news. Only two men now remained, John Adams and Thomas Jefferson. It was up to these two to decide who would write the Declaration of Independence, the document that would state why America believed it should be free.

Seated at a round oak table, Adams and Jefferson stared at one another in stubborn silence. Though they agreed on what the document should say, they could not agree on one very important point—who should write it. The Declaration would set out the philosophy and ideals of the new nation, America, and its phrases would travel far beyond Philadelphia. Each man insisted that the other would be better.

Thomas Jefferson of Virginia was one of the youngest men in Congress. He had only recently become involved in politics. John Adams, the delegate from Mas-

Adams and Jefferson decide who should write the Declaration.

sachusetts, had years of experience. Jefferson thought it was only logical that the task of writing this important document should fall to the older, more experienced statesman.

"*I will not!*" Adams replied bluntly. John Adams scowled and crossed his arms over his broad chest. He had made up his mind that Jefferson should do it and, as all his friends knew, once John Adams set his mind on something it was impossible to change it.

"But why, John? I don't understand," Jefferson asked. He was also a firm man, but always calm and almost never raised his voice.

"Reasons enough," the short man huffed.

Jefferson, who was tall with wavy red hair, tried to hold back a smile at Adams's remarkably stubborn behavior. "Name one," Jefferson challenged him.

"I have many," the older man replied. "The most important one, however, is that *you* are by far the better writer."

It was true that young Thomas Jefferson had become known for his writing. In Virginia, he had written a paper about the rights of America, rights which he felt England had ignored. He wrote it for members of the Virginia delegation to read to the first Continental Congress, but his friends had extra copies printed up. Before long, Jefferson's paper was being read all over America, and even in England. John Adams had read and greatly admired Jefferson's paper. Adams was convinced that Thomas Jefferson was the perfect person to write the Declaration of Independence.

At last Jefferson was persuaded. "I will do it," he told Adams with a firm nod of his head. "It will be difficult . . . but I will do the best job that I can."

Adams's plump, stern face lit up with a smile. "Good!" he said. "When you have drawn it up, we will meet to look it over before showing it to the other delegates." With that, he gathered up his papers and left.

In his room, Thomas sat down by the window and began to consider the enormous job he had taken on. Was he the right man to compose this important document?

Today, we all know about Thomas Jefferson. He was one of the first great thinkers of America. As a writer,

"In his own room, Thomas sat down by the window."

an inventor, a statesman, and an architect he explored the new ideas about science and government that were taking shape all around him. Everyone knows that he became president of the United States. And today, most people know that he wrote the Declaration of Independence. But we rarely think of how the young man felt that afternoon, sitting alone in his room, about to begin the greatest challenge of his life.

The Congress gave Thomas Jefferson two weeks to write the Declaration. They wanted him to state clearly that from now on, Americans refused to obey English law. With this document, the colonies were declaring themselves independent. Americans would govern themselves.

This in itself was an enormous job, but Thomas set himself an even harder goal. He felt it wasn't enough to simply declare that America would be free. He wanted to explain the principle that the new country would be founded on, the belief that all people—not only Americans—had a right to freedom.

Thomas had first learned the principle of individual freedom as a student in Williamsburg. He had learned that there were certain rights that all people had—to live, to be able to make their own choices, to be free to do as they wished as long as it didn't hurt others. Today we take these ideas for granted, but they were fairly new in the 1770's. Not everyone believed in them, or even thought much about them. Thomas Jefferson did. His teachers said that Thomas was their most thoughtful student.

Thomas had seen that the British rulers of America were not granting the colonists their basic rights as individuals. The Americans were not allowed to govern themselves, to set taxes for themselves, or to defend themselves. Each year, disputes between England and the colonies over these ideas had grown more serious.

King George, sitting in his magnificent palace in London, did not understand the American colonists. How dare they challenge his rule over them? To King George, the American colonists were British subjects. The Americans wanted to make their own laws, or at least have some voice in the British government that ruled over them. King George would not even consider that possibility. The colonists would have to fight for their freedom. Now it was up to him, Thomas Jefferson of Virginia, to take America's first and boldest step towards independence.

As Thomas sat looking out the window at the sunny Philadelphia streets, his thoughts wandered. He tried to concentrate on writing the Declaration, but worries over family matters distracted him. He wondered about his dear wife, Martha, far away in Virginia. She had been very sick, and it took a week or more for letters from his family to reach him. Had she recovered? Was she worse? Wondering about Martha drove him nearly crazy. Thomas also thought about his mother, who had died only three months before. He was still full of sadness over her death.

Thomas put down his pen and leaned back in his chair. Outside, the street was teeming with people: men carrying lumber on their shoulders; women strolling with frilly parasols to protect their faces from the sun; dirty-faced boys and girls dashing through the markets.

Gazing upon life in the city, Thomas Jefferson thought back to his childhood days in the lush, green Virginia countryside. How different his life had been as a boy, living at the very edge of the wilderness. In his wildest childhood dreams, had he ever imagined that events would lead him to such a momentous time?

CHAPTER TWO

Virginia Boy

One crisp autumn morning, young Thomas and his father hiked to the top of a mountain called Pantops near their home. It was the highest point for many miles around, and the view from its peak was breathtaking. As they neared the very top, Thomas hurried up the narrow path ahead of his father.

Although the sight was familiar to him, Thomas always felt exhilarated staring down at the valley from such a height. As the morning's mist burned away, he could see the rich red soil of the Virginia farmlands. Planted in neat squares of green tobacco crops, the valley looked like a vast patchwork quilt. The Rivanna River flowed through the farmlands and hills like a big snake. Far in the distance, Thomas could see the plantations of Dr. Walker and John Harvie, the Jefferson family's closest neighbors.

As usual, Thomas was full of questions for his father this morning. "How far does your land reach, Father? Show me again."

With a patient smile his father pointed out the plantation's boundaries.

"Have you ever ridden past those mountains?"

Thomas asked, pointing to the West. "Will you take me with you next time you go?"

"Perhaps when you are older, Thomas." His father laughed and ruffled his son's red hair. "We can ride to those mountains, and beyond them. To places no one has ever set foot before."

Peter Jefferson was an important man in Virginia. He owned a large plantation and made money by growing tobacco, which was sold to England. He was also a well-known explorer and mapmaker who had charted much of the Virginia wilderness. Peter Jefferson's tales of adventure in the wilderness made Thomas long to become an explorer, too. Thomas dreamed of charting the furthest, most untamed territories when he grew up, places where no one had ever set foot before.

Virginia was one of thirteen British colonies in America. There were some disputes between the Americans and their British rulers, but usually they were settled peacefully. The governor, an Englishman, met with Peter Jefferson and other landowners when there was a change in taxes or laws.

Thomas knew very little about England when he was growing up. He knew the King of England ruled over them, but the problems his father sometimes mentioned seemed slight, and England seemed too far away to matter.

Thomas's first home was the family plantation of Shadwell on the Rivanna River. Peter Jefferson chose the name because his wife was born in a part of England called Shadwell, and he wanted to make her feel at home.

When Thomas was only two years old, the family moved to a plantation owned by another family, the Randolphs. Mr. Randolph had recently died and since Peter Jefferson was his good friend, he had promised to help take care of the Randolph children.

Thomas had four sisters—two older and two younger. His older sister Jane was his favorite. The Randolphs' plantation was big and there were always plenty of things to do. He was lucky to have so many other children around, for Virginia plantations could be lonely. The farms were huge and neighbors were miles away. Thomas's favorite game was hide-and-seek. He was clever at thinking up new places to hide. Once, he hid inside a big pot in the kitchen. Another time, he used leafy branches to make a nest in a tree so that no one on the ground could see him. The other children searched everywhere and finally gave up. Thomas did not come out from his hiding place, because he had brought one of his father's books with him. He was quite content to sit high in the tree, watching the clouds, reading, and imagining faraway lands.

When Tom was nine years old his family moved from the Randolphs' place back to their own plantation, Shadwell. Peter Jefferson had decided that the Randolph children were old enough to take care of themselves. His duty to his friend was done. He was eager to get back to his own farm.

Tom was never so excited as on the day the wagons rolled up to the gates at Shadwell. He was too young to remember it and the idea of having a new house, a new bedroom window to look out of, and new things to explore outside was so thrilling he couldn't sit still.

Since Jane was three years older than Tom, she remembered Shadwell and was happy to be home. She took her little brother all around the plantation and showed him everything. It wasn't as big as the Randolphs' place, but it was new to Tom and everything was different.

The river was close to the house, just down the hill, and Tom and Jane liked to run down the hill, faster and faster, and then stop just at the water's edge. Near the house were other buildings to explore: the dairy, where the cows were milked, and the smokehouse, where meat was cured.

Children in that time were lucky because they could see for themselves how things were made—things like cheese and butter and barrels. Nearly everything was made right at home. Thomas asked questions about each step in each process:

"How does milk become cheese?"

"Why does smoke keep meat from going bad?"

"Will smoked meat last forever?"

His father encouraged him to ask questions, and made sure that Tom learned all he could teach, for these skills were important for every man to have. Tom asked questions about everything he saw. His sister Jane told him that the workers moved the crops every two year, and that after tobacco was in a field for two years they planted Indian corn the next year. Tom asked why, but she didn't know. So he asked William, the man in charge of the tobacco. William told them that the tobacco plants

11

took nutrients out of the soil, that after two years the soil wouldn't grow healthy plants anymore. The tobacco had to be moved to another part of the plantation. Then corn was planted in the old fields to give the soil a rest.

Tom learned all of the secrets of making things on the farm. He learned how to make a round barrel using flat pieces of wood, how to turn cream into butter, even how to make ink out of walnut shells and vinegar!

Thomas's father was a surveyor as well as an explorer. A surveyor measures a piece of land so that buildings can be built on it. Much of Virginia was unsettled wilderness and surveying was important work. Land is almost never perfectly flat. A surveyor has to figure out how to build on or around hills. When the land was surveyed, more people could come and build their houses and, eventually, new towns in these uninhabited places. Thomas liked the idea of being a surveyor and helping people settle new territories. Surveying tools measure such things as how steep a hill is, and Peter Jefferson taught his son how to use them. One day, Thomas told himself he would join his father and explore the mysterious lands of the vast West.

Thomas's sister Jane wanted to learn too, but her father scoffed at the idea. "It's simply not proper for a woman to do such work, Jane," he said. Thomas was sorry that Jane couldn't learn how to be a surveyor. He thought it would be fun for them to travel together to strange new places when they were older. He was sure she would be a good explorer. She loved to hike through the hills with him, no matter how rough or steep the

Tom and Jane liked to go to the very peak of Pantops.

climb. Even to the very peak of Pantops. High above the Virginia Valley, Jane and Thomas would tell each other their special dreams about the future.

Thomas's dream was to become a famous explorer, to help expand the country and make life better for the hard-working settlers. Someday, his dream would come true. But not in a way he ever imagined.

Thomas's father was often away, charting new lands. When he came home, it was like a holiday. The family would have a big feast. Afterwards, they would sit around the fireplace and Thomas and his older sister Jane would beg their father to tell them stories of his travels. Once Peter Jefferson told them how he'd almost been killed one day while riding down a steep mountain. His horse had stumbled and he fell in front of the frightened animal's hooves. He managed to roll out of the way in the nick of time.

Tom and Jane loved to hear how their father and his companions often met up with wild animals, like bears, mountain lions and snakes. The explorers often slept in trees at night as protection against the wild creatures. "I'd love to sleep up in the trees," Jane said. "Tomorrow, Tom and I will build a tree house and we'll never sleep in a plain old bed again."

CHAPTER THREE

Off to School

Thomas had his heart set on becoming an explorer and surveyor, but Peter Jefferson had other plans for his son. He wanted him to go to school and get a proper education. His dream was to see Thomas grow up to become a Virginia gentleman.

A gentleman in those days meant much more than it does today. It meant someone who was in a higher class than most people, someone who had more money and education. Today "gentleman" is a polite way to say "a man." But then only someone who owned land could be called a gentleman. Even after the Revolution, only "gentlemen" were allowed to vote. This meant that no women could vote, and no men who didn't own a certain amount of land.

So you can see that Thomas Jefferson was lucky. His father could afford to send him to school.

On a bright September morning in 1752, a wagon drove up the path to Shadwell. The driver gave a shout and the family hurried outside. Everyone helped load Thomas's bags into the coach. His mother fussed over him before he left and told him he must write once a week, telling them everything he had learned. Jane hugged him and said she was proud of her little brother.

His father gave him a present: an expensive Latin dictionary that had come all the way from England. It was a big book with a purple cover with gold lettering. Thomas bowed and thanked him shyly. The present made him feel old. The driver called, and he jumped into the wagon. He smiled at his family as the wagon pulled away to show them he was happy, but inside he felt nervous and frightened.

The school was in a town called Northam. It had only one teacher, Reverend Douglas. Thomas lived with him and his family in their house. Everything in his life was different now . . . and Thomas was completely miserable! He couldn't get used to the Douglas family, who were stern and serious.

Thomas tried to pay attention to his studies, but the classes were so boring they nearly drove him to tears. He was studying Latin and Greek, which all young gentlemen needed to learn because the great early books were written in one of those languages. Thomas was curious about the strange languages and the big books that lined the walls of Rev. Douglas's study, but he never got to read them. Instead, Rev. Douglas gave his students hour after hour of grammar drills, making them repeat nouns and verbs until they thought they would go crazy.

The boys also had to study manners. Rev. Douglas had a special book that they had to memorize. Here is some of what they learned:

Bite not thy bread, but break it, but not with slovenly fingers, nor with the same wherewith thou takest up thy meat.

Spit not, cough not, nor blow thy nose at table if it may be avoided; but if there be necessity, do it aside, and without much noise.

Stuff not thy mouth so as to fill thy cheeks.

Blow not thy meat, but with patience wait till it be cool.

Thomas stayed at school for five years. During that whole time the only fun he had was when he got to go home for summer vacation. Shadwell was a busy place in those days. His father was a prominent man in the county and there were lots of visitors—other farmers, surveyors, and sometimes traveling salesmen. Thomas liked to sit on the porch when the salesmen came and listen as they talked about faraway places and events, about shipwrecks off the coast of Maryland, bear hunters in the woods of Pennsylvania, and the price of tobacco in London.

The summer always ended too quickly. Reluctantly, Thomas would pack up and return to Rev. Douglas's school. One day in his fifth year at school, not long after he'd been back from summer vacation, he was having lunch at the Douglas's big wooden table with the other boys, and he looked up to see his sister Jane walk into the room. He jumped up, excited and confused.

"Jane!" he cried. "What in the world are you doing here?"

Jane curtseyed and said "Pardon me" to Rev. Douglas and his wife. Tom saw that she had been crying.

"Tom," she said softly, "you must come home right away. Father has died."

Thomas stared at her. Tears came into his eyes, but he told himself he was too old to cry. He excused himself from the table and walked over and put his arms around his sister. They walked out onto the porch. Then they both wept together.

Thomas returned home at once, feeling numb and confused. He didn't know what to do. How could his father have died? He had always been so strong, so lively. He felt hollow inside. Mrs. Jefferson and the children sat together in front of the fire and comforted each other.

There were eight children in the family now. Besides Thomas, Jane and Mary there were five younger ones: Elizabeth, Martha, Lucy, Anna, and Randolph, Thomas's only brother. Anna and Randolph were twins. They were only two years old, so Thomas and his older sisters would have to help their mother take care of them. There was also so much work to be done on the plantation. Thomas would have to take over the job of managing everything.

Then he thought of his father's last words. As he lay dying, Peter Jefferson told his wife that Tom was not to return to Shadwell to work on the farm. He was to continue studying, to get the best education possible. He wanted her to make Tom promise to do this.

So, sitting on the mountaintop and looking out across the lush green valley, Thomas promised his father that he would study and learn, and whatever he was going to do in the future, he would do it as best he could. With great sadness he realized that he would never explore the wilderness with his father as he had dreamed of doing.

After his father's death, Thomas changed schools. It was the first decision he had ever made on his own, and he never regretted it.

His new teacher was Reverend Maury. Under his guidance, Thomas quickly learned how much he had been missing in Rev. Douglas's classes. Now he loved his classes and worked hard at them. He was also happy because the school was close to Shadwell. Each Saturday he rode his slow pony home for the weekend, full of exciting new facts to tell Jane.

He also had a best friend now, a boy about the same age, named Dabney Carr. But the two boys didn't start out as friends.

One day not long after Tom started going to school, Dabney Carr, a strong boy whom the others looked up to, was sitting outside with eleven-year-old James Maury, Rev. Maury's son. They saw Thomas Jefferson come riding up the road on his slow pony. Suddenly Dabney burst out laughing.

"What's so funny?" James asked.

Dabney pointed to Tom's pony. "That old beast is slower than a turtle with a broken leg!" he cried, and laughed harder.

Tom heard this. "My pony can ride fast when I want it to," he said coldly. This wasn't true—Tom's pony was an old crippled thing—but the other boy's laughing made him so mad he was determined to prove him wrong.

Dabney laughed again and immediately challenged Tom to a race. Tom accepted, but when he saw Dabney's horse—a beautiful animal, big and sleek—he knew he had made a mistake. There was no way in the world Tom could win. But he refused to give in. He thought hard about what he could do.

Suddenly a smile spread across his face. He said he'd be happy to race Dabney, but that he wouldn't do it until the end of the month. It was February, and Tom said the race would be held on February 30. Dabney agreed, saying that Tom was only delaying his defeat. The two boys shook hands.

It wasn't until the last day of the month, February 28, that Dabney realized Tom had tricked him. February, of course, only has twenty-eight days. Since there is no such day as February 30, there could never be a race. Tom expected Dabney to be really mad, but to his surprise, Dabney laughed when he realized the trick. He said that Tom Jefferson was the smartest kid he knew. He put his arm around Tom's shoulder, and from then on they were best friends.

With Rev. Maury Thomas studied Latin and Greek again, but this time he was really interested. Rev. Maury encouraged the boys to read the ancient stories and ask questions about the languages. It fascinated Thomas that these languages were so old and so different from English, but that English contained many Latin and Greek words and pieces of words. He loved to examine words, like a scientist examines a substance under a microscope.

Take, for example, the word *school*. Believe it or not, the Greek word "schole" (which is pretty similar) actually meant "vacation"! The Greeks thought that you could only study when you weren't busy working, when you were on holiday, so their word for "vacation" is the same as our word "school."

Many words have strange histories like this, and that's why Thomas Jefferson loved learning about them. And he studied very hard: his family later said that Thomas studied fifteen hours a day when he was in school! Maybe for the Greeks school was a vacation, but not for Thomas Jefferson.

The more he learned, the more he wanted to know. He became intensely curious about not only the things he was studying in school but everything around him, too. He wanted to dig to the roots of things, to find out what made them work, why they were the way they were and not different.

But most of all he was fascinated by the ideas he was learning. It was his father who had made him want to be an explorer, but he wasn't thinking about exploring the wilderness so much anymore. He wanted to explore ideas. He liked what Rev. Maury taught him and, without realizing it, he was becoming a real student. He no longer wanted to just go back to the farm.

And by the time he left Rev. Maury he knew what he wanted to do next: attend college at William and Mary in Williamsburg, the capital of the colony of Virginia.

CHAPTER FOUR

Learning the Way

Williamsburg was a small city, but a noble one. Its main street was one hundred feet wide and a mile long. At one end stood the Capitol Building, where the gentlemen of Virginia raised their voices in political speeches. At the other end was William and Mary College.

Tom entered the college when he was seventeen. William and Mary is still a college today, but in those days it was quite different. There were only about one hundred people all together—including teachers and students. There was a regular college, which Tom attended, and there was the Divinity School (for people studying to be ministers), the Grammar School (for boys too young for college), and there was even an Indian School, where Indians could learn to read and write.

Most colleges today have rules that the students must follow. Here are some of the rules that Thomas and the other students had to obey:

- no student was allowed to keep racehorses
- no student was allowed to bet on billiards or other games
- no student was allowed to have cards or dice

Williamsburg was a small city.

- it was forbidden to "tell a lie or curse or swear, or talk or do any thing obscene, or quarrel and fight, or play at cards or dice, or set in to drinking or do any thing else that is contrary to good manners"

You might think that with so many rules all the students at the college were very good and that there was never trouble. But you'd be wrong. One night not long after Tom arrived some of the students got into a fight with the boys from the town of Williamsburg. And, incredible as it may seem, it was two of the teachers from the college who led the students in the fight!

The two teachers were fired, and since it wasn't easy to find other teachers, Thomas's math teacher, a man named William Small, took over all the subjects. So Dr. Small was just about the only teacher Thomas had, and this was the luckiest thing that had ever happened to him. Dr. Small, as it turned out, was a truly great teacher. He didn't just make his students memorize facts. He was familiar with the new ideas and discoveries of writers and scientists in Europe, and in his lessons, he introduced this new world to his students.

Thomas learned from Dr. Small that science was not only interesting, but that it could actually help people. This was a new idea—people had studied science before, but most of them treated it as a kind of game; they had never tried to really use it. Now Tom learned how French, English, and Italian men had put scientific principles to work to explain how the planets moved and to create tools—accurate clocks, eyeglasses, microscopes—that would help men to live better lives.

Dr. Small also taught his students that it was important for every person to think for himself. Before, when people had wanted to learn how something worked, they looked for the answer in books, or in religion, or they asked older, wiser men. But scientists looked for answers in the world. Dr. Small taught that science worked because it relied upon the ability of people to *reason*. Reason is when a person uses his mind like a tool to examine the world and search for answers. The thinkers of the time believed reason was the most powerful tool in the world. By using it, they thought, people could eventually find answers to everything.

Thomas learned how the greatest of all European scientists, Sir Isaac Newton, had discovered the most important principles of science by applying reason to his observations.

Newton knew that people didn't have a good understanding of the way the world worked. Take apples, for example. Before Newton, everyone thought they knew all about apples. If an apple broke off a branch, it would fall down. Everyone knew that because they had seen it happen lots of times.

But Newton wasn't content. He began to reason, to examine the problem in his mind. He asked himself questions:

Why does an apple fall down? Why doesn't it fall up? Why doesn't it just stay in the air?

Newton decided that there must be a force that attracts things to the earth, and he called the force "gravity."

Next he thought about the moon. Everyone knew the moon moved around the earth, but they weren't sure why. Suddenly it came to Newton that gravity must also work in space. He realized that the moon moves around the earth for the same reason that apples fall down: gravity.

By reasoning, he had discovered an important force that operates in the world.

The use of reason was so simple and so powerful that it held Tom in a kind of trance. It matched his natural curiosity perfectly. He became on fire now, studying and reading and reasoning day and night, eager to explore. The whole world seemed to open up to him.

He was, after all, very much like his father. For him, doing was better than just thinking. And so as he learned new ideas he experimented with them, to think of how they could be used in everyday life. Back at Shadwell over vacations, he invented a plow that tilled the earth more efficiently and he came up with an improved system of crop rotation.

His greatest experiment would come later, when he would use these ideas to help build a government. Now he could only vaguely imagine where his exploration would lead, but he felt certain that these ideas would help to make the world of the future a better place.

All his life, Thomas was grateful for his early introduction to scientific thinking. Years later, when he was an old man, he said that having Dr. Small as a teacher had "probably fixed the destinies of my life."

While Thomas was at college he met many new people, and he had some old friends there too. Dabney Carr came a year after he did (still riding a nice horse), and the two immediately took to studying and talking together, discussing not only science and law but a new subject as well: girls.

Thomas was now becoming very concerned about his looks. He knew he wasn't a very good-looking young man. He was tall—over six feet—and had red hair that would never stay down, and his arms and legs were long and awkward. And the thing that really bothered him was his feet—they were so big that whenever he went to a party he always felt that all the girls were staring at them. Still, he met some girls, and they always liked him because he knew a lot about so many new things, and he was very formal and complimented them, saying their hair was very beautiful and so on. But he was usually too shy to talk, and in those days a man always had to speak to the lady first, so he didn't talk much with women.

And then he developed a new passion that made him forget about girls for a while. He began learning about European architecture. He bought a book with pictures of magnificent buildings in Italy. The more he read, the more excited he became. He wanted to explore the grand ideas of architecture that stretched back to Greece and Rome, the great ages of mankind that he loved so much to read about. And the more he learned, the more ashamed he felt that there were no buildings in America that could match the great ones of Europe. He decided that he would become a great builder.

One day he went back to Shadwell and announced that he was going to build a great house.

His mother had gotten used to her son's habit of planning something new every time he read about a new idea, so she didn't ask why he wanted to build a house, and she didn't bother telling him that he didn't know enough about architecture yet. She knew he would learn what he needed to know. But she did want to know where he would build it. "Will it be right here, at Shadwell?" she asked.

Thomas shook his head. "No, I'll build up on Little

Mountain," he said. "That's the grandest spot for miles around. It's the perfect place for a house." He even had a name picked out for the new house. It was going to be called Monticello, which meant "little mountain" in Italian.

Full of energy, he set about having the land at Little Mountain cleared. He did the surveying himself, using the tools that his father had given him when he died.

But he couldn't devote much time to the house just then, because his first obligation was to his studies in Williamsburg. His classes with Dr. Small were nearly finished, but he had decided that he was going to become a lawyer, which meant more studying.

Back in Williamsburg, Thomas moved into a house in town. He had two roommates. John Tyler was a hardworking student, like him. They were both always at their books. However, the other roommate, Frank Willis, was not a hard worker at all. Sometimes he would come home late at night after a party and get so fed up at seeing the other two still studying that he'd flip over the table, scattering their books and papers all over the floor. John would shout at Frank Willis that he was never going to become a lawyer if he didn't study. Thomas would just shake his head and go back to his books.

He wasn't always studying. Life in Williamsburg was very exciting for a young law student. There were parties to go to and new people to meet. And even though it was a city of only three hundred houses, it was still the largest place he had ever been! What's more, it was the center of Virginia's government and the home of the governor.

At the parties he met other young men studying law whose fathers were plantation owners, and he met politicians who worked in the House of Burgesses, the colony's governing body. And, since it was such a small town, it wasn't long before he met the governor himself at a party. After a while they even became friends.

He also began to learn about politics. He was beginning to see that there were problems between the colony and the "mother country."

The governor—a small, lively Englishman who loved music and conversation more than politics—took Thomas aside and explained that the problems would be solved soon. Most of them were small, he said, nothing to worry about. Thomas believed him, and he didn't think about it again until one day in 1765, when Thomas Jefferson was twenty-two. On that day, he heard a speech in the House of Burgesses that changed his life.

CHAPTER FIVE

Rights in Action

"Treason! Treason!" The members of the Virginia Assembly in the House of Burgesses came to their feet. "The man speaks treason against our king!" They were horrified at the words of Patrick Henry, who was speaking out against England's right to rule the colony.

Thomas strained to hear Henry's voice over the angry shouts. He didn't want to miss a single word. Thomas and his roommate John Tyler often went to the House of Burgesses to hear the speakers. It was a good way to learn about law in action. Patrick Henry's speech was by far the boldest address he'd ever heard there.

Thomas had met Patrick Henry five years before. Patrick, who was older, already had a wife and children. Even though they didn't have much in common, Thomas and Patrick Henry got along well. Patrick was a rough, plain-talking mountain man, but he was honest and sincere in his beliefs. Thomas, the hard-working student, careful in his speech and dress, took an instant liking to him. Patrick Henry had a simple, friendly manner that Thomas admired.

Since their last meeting, Patrick Henry had become a lawyer even though Thomas could never figure out how he did it. Thomas had studied many years to become a lawyer, but Patrick claimed he had done it in six weeks! Now as a new member of the Assembly, Patrick was becoming famous for his direct style of speaking and his strong ideas.

All afternoon the members had been discussing a new tax that England had just declared Americans would have to pay. Of course, all governments have taxes and even if people don't like to pay them, there is usually a good reason for them. But many of the colonists could not see the purpose of the new tax the English Parliament had declared. This new tax forced Americans to buy a stamp to put on all writing that was done in the colonies. Every time one Virginian wrote a letter to another, it would have to be stamped. Every newspaper that was sold in the colonies would also have to be stamped, and the money from the stamps would go to England.

Americans were outraged about the Stamp Act. England had no right to make money from business that took place within the colonies! But the real problem, Thomas thought, was that England was not letting the Americans have a fair say in the laws that they had to obey. The English Parliament had ruled without hearing the American side.

The colonists were angry, but they were still British subjects, and King George was their king. They didn't like the new tax, but they were a long way from talking about revolution. That wouldn't happen for another eleven years.

But one man wasn't afraid to take a stand. As

Patrick Henry protests the Stamp Act.

Thomas Jefferson and his friend leaned forward in the lobby to hear better, Patrick Henry stood up and began to speak. He was a striking figure. Tall and lean, he always wore the buckskin shirt of a mountain man. Thomas paid no attention to Patrick Henry's appearance, however. Instead he listened to Patrick Henry's words, feeling as if he was hearing his own thoughts—thoughts he had not spoken to anyone yet.

The English were using America the way people use a tool, Patrick Henry said. They didn't care for Americans, their rights, their laws. They only cared about making money from the colonies. He paused, his dark eyes flashing. Then he began again, his voice rising even higher. Every member of the Virginia Assembly sat horrified as Patrick Henry stood before them and declared that King George—their king—ought to be put to death.

Actually, Patrick Henry didn't say it exactly like that, but in a much more clever way. He said, "Caesar had his Brutus" (Caesar was a Roman emperor, killed by Brutus) and that King Charles of England had his Cromwell (Cromwell killed King Charles.) And then he said, "And George the Third. . . ."

But he didn't finish. For all the Assembly members leaped to their feet, shouting, "Treason! Treason!"

After all, Mr. Henry was talking about murdering their king! But Patrick Henry quickly finished his sentence: "King George . . . may profit by their example."

The members were still in an uproar. No one had ever spoken out against England so strongly. Many were young however, and fired up by Patrick Henry's speech. His voice still ringing through the rafters, Henry proposed that they vote to officially deny English Parliament the right to tax them. Caught up in his powerful words, the members agreed.

Standing in the lobby with John Tyler, Thomas could hardly believe what he had seen and heard. The House of Burgesses, swept up by Patrick Henry's stirring plea for American rights, had officially declared that it would not accept British control! It was an important moment in the slow, but sure movement towards revolution. For the first time, the colony of Virginia was telling England that it would decide a matter on its own.

Thomas looked around, as the Assembly members chattered excitedly. What would happen now, he wondered.

Alone in his room that night, Thomas finished his studying and stared out at the starry sky. His thoughts returned to Patrick Henry's speech. He could recall every word. Somehow Thomas knew that after this day, things would never be the same in Virginia. He would never be the same either. In Dr. Small's class he had learned how reason could solve all problems. In a flash, Thomas understood that abstract ideas he had learned from Dr. Small were actually very real and of great importance, not only to Virginians, but to people everywhere. He realized that if he examined the problems of America and England logically, it was all a matter of rights. He saw that Americans—and all people—had a right to make their own laws and decisions. For England to tax Americans without allowing them to represent themselves in the English Parliament, was simply wrong. There was nothing for the colonists to do but declare that Parliament was being unfair. They should refuse to go along with laws they considered unjust.

Today, we would say that of course all people have a right to make their own laws. But this belief was fairly new at the time. Suddenly it all made sense to Thomas. He knew what was the real problem between England and America, and he knew what needed to be done to solve it.

Soon everyone in Williamsburg was talking about Patrick Henry's speech. In the shops, in the homes of both rich and poor, at the college, in the pubs, and even in the churches, people asked one another, "What will happen now?"

Thomas joined in the discussions. He told people what he thought, and when they heard how clearly he understood the issues—and saw that he had obviously given these problems much thought—they listened to him carefully.

One afternoon, Thomas and his friends were gathered at his home. Talk turned to America's problems with England. John Tyler came into the room carrying a letter. "Here, Tom, this is for you," he said.

Thomas eagerly tore the envelope open. He was always happy to hear news of his family. The other young men continued their discussion. Suddenly, they noticed Thomas had grown completely silent. He was staring blankly ahead of him.

"What's wrong?" one whispered. "Thomas? What is it? Tell us what's happened."

Thomas could hardly speak. "It's my sister . . . Jane," he said finally. "She's dead . . ." Then he hid his face in his hands.

As soon as Thomas learned the terrible news, he left for Shadwell. When he arrived home he learned that no one really knew how Jane died. She was very young, only three years older than Thomas. She might have died from an illness that would be curable today, perhaps pneumonia or the flu, but in the hills of Virginia at that time, medical help was very limited.

Jane's death was an enormous shock to Thomas. He felt sadder than he could remember feeling since his father had died so many years earlier. He and his older sister had always been so close; more than brother and sister, they had been the best of friends.

"It is hard to believe that Jane will never again be here to greet me on the porch when I return home to Shadwell," he told his mother one day, "or to ask me questions about my studies, or to sing while I play the violin."

His mother nodded sadly. She understood her son's grief. Jane's death had left an empty place in both of their lives. Shadwell was never quite the same without her. His older sister, Mary, was married and lived with her husband. His younger sister Martha had recently married also—to none other than Tom's old friend Dabney Carr. At Shadwell, there was now only his mother, his sisters Elizabeth and Lucy, and the ten-year-old twins, Anna and Randolph.

Thomas knew it was his duty to stay at Shadwell and take care of the farm. Because he felt very lonely, he put all his energy into his work on the farm.

He began to make very detailed records of nearly everything that happened on the farm. He was to continue this practice all his life. In his record books he wrote that a horse ate eight to ten bundles of feed a night, and a coach with six horses needs eighty feet of room to turn around in. He even labeled plots of ground for farming, and numbered the rows in each plot, and sometimes he went so far as to number each plant!

Once the farm was organized, Thomas returned to Williamsburg. In the next year, 1767, he finished his studies and finally became a lawyer. Thomas Jefferson is known today as many things—president, secretary of state, governor of Virginia—but he isn't so well known as a lawyer. Yet, during almost eight years, he had 949 law cases. Some of them were important, some not so important. In one case his client accused another man of breaking into his house and stealing a bottle of whisky and a shirt!

As he became a well-known lawyer he became more and more interested in defending people who were not treated fairly, whose rights were violated. He worked without getting paid in such cases, and in time he developed a reputation as a "lawyer of the people."

One day a black man, a slave, came into Thomas Jefferson's office. His name was Samuel Howell. He said he needed a lawyer because he wanted to go to court to win his freedom. Samuel Howell believed that under Virginia law he was entitled to be a free man because his great-grandmother was white. Other lawyers had refused to talk to him. Samuel Howell explained to Thomas, "They said I have no rights."

Thomas Jefferson eagerly took the case. He put all his energy into preparing a strong argument. His argument was not based on Virginia law, though, but on his own reasoning. He did not argue that Samuel Howell should be free because he was partly white. Instead, he shocked the court by saying that Virginia's laws were not important at all.

"What do you mean by that, Mr. Jefferson?" the judge asked, his face red with anger.

"I mean, Your Honor, that the law of nature is more important than the law of Virginia," Thomas declared. "And under that law, we are all born free."

The whole courtroom was stunned. Not only was this young lawyer defending a slave, but he had the nerve to argue that all slaves had a right to be free!

Many people at that time felt that slavery was an unjust institution, but nobody did anything to stop it. In fact, many white people who owned slaves believed that it was wrong. Thomas Jefferson himself was one of these; he had fifty slaves at Shadwell.

It's strange that people who didn't believe in slavery would still own slaves, but many did. The problem was that farming was the most important industry in the South. Since there were no machines to pick cotton and tobacco, the farms and plantations depended on slaves. Without them, the whole economy of the South would fall apart. So, while many Southerners thought slavery was wrong, they depended on it.

Even before Thomas Jefferson finished his argument, the court had made up its mind. There was no way they would free this man. Samuel Howell, they ruled, must remain a slave.

Thomas was furious at the court's decision. He determined to try again. In 1769, he became a member of the Virginia House of Burgesses. His first official action was to propose a law that would let a man free his own slaves if he wanted to. It was actually against the law at that time for someone to free his own slaves, and Thomas thought that if this were changed it would be the first step toward abolishing slavery in America. But, believe it or not, the House of Burgesses voted strongly against Jefferson's proposal.

Thomas was heartsick. He and all the other wealthy white men of Virginia were going against the very laws of nature that he believed in so strongly. Americans were willing to stand up to the English because the English were violating their rights. But they were not yet willing to see that they themselves were violating the rights of their slaves, Thomas thought sadly.

CHAPTER SIX

What a House Is

Thomas often rode to Charlottesville on business. One cold evening in February, after a long day in court, he was sitting in the common room of a guesthouse, chatting with a few other patrons in front of a cheerful fire. All of a sudden Jupiter, one of the servants at Shadwell, came rushing in. Thomas thought back to the day his sister Jane had appeared at Rev. Douglas's school. In a panic he asked what was wrong.

"There's been a fire at Shadwell," Jupiter said. Thomas jumped up.

"Is anyone hurt?" he cried.

"No," Jupiter said, "everyone's just fine."

Thomas relaxed. Then he started again. His books! He had been collecting books for a long time, starting with the small collection his father had willed to him.

"Did they save my books?"

Jupiter shook his head sadly. "No, Master," he said. "All lost." Then he smiled. "But we saved your fiddle!" he cried, thinking Thomas would care more about this than his books.

Thomas rode back to Shadwell and surveyed the damage. Much of the house was ruined. His entire collection of books and all of his legal papers and notes were gone.

The loss was terrible. Books were extremely hard to get in the colonies and Thomas considered them his most valuable possession. He wrote to a friend: "I calculate the cost of the books to have been two hundred sterling. Would to God it had been the money; then it had never cost me a sigh!"

After the fire he fell into a black mood. For days he would talk to no one. The family set about rebuilding Shadwell. Thomas directed the work, but his heart wasn't in it.

Then one day he happened to gaze up toward the other house, the one he was building on Little Mountain—Monticello. "I'm going to move into the new house right away," he told his family that night.

"But Thomas, it's not even close to being finished," his mother said. "How can you live there?"

"I will manage as best as I can," Thomas replied. "Perhaps living there will help me to work on it faster."

"Perhaps," his mother said quietly. She already knew that her son liked to work out his problems in unusual ways. If living in a half-finished house would make him happy, she wasn't going to argue against it. She suspected that such a change might even lift his spirits. And she was right. Soon everyone saw a complete change in Thomas. He smiled and whistled as he worked—seeming almost happy that there had been a fire. Everyone tried to help him with the work on Monticello. Friends sent useful supplies such as hinges, pulleys, and ropes. One friend, who knew that Thomas wanted to plant a fruit orchard at his new house, even sent apricots and grapevines.

As the house took shape, Thomas's smile became brighter still. Ever since he and his sister, Jane, used to sit on Pantops and look out at Little Mountain, he had wanted to build a home there. Now he could see it take shape before his very eyes.

It seemed magical, that you could draw something out on paper and then watch as it grew in space. It gave him a feeling of power. He thought how wonderful it was that humans had such power over nature; he could picture something in his mind, then using the materials of nature make his creation come alive. It was like making a beautiful sculpture. Only it was even better, because it wasn't just something to look at, but a place to live. It would protect him and his family, keep them warm and safe.

And, of course, he did it himself. Most people would call in an expert if they wanted to build a house, but Thomas Jefferson believed that people should think for themselves, not just follow what others said. All his life he loved to explore. His father had explored the wilderness, and Thomas explored ideas. So when it came to building a house, he was determined to do it himself. He wanted to explore all the possibilities.

He had several ideas about what his house should be like. For one, it should be able to change. After all, people change year by year. Thomas believed a house should change with the people who live in it. As a family grows and changes, so should their home.

He also wanted Monticello to be a stately house, very proper and formal, with columns on the porch (such as are on the White House today) and a dome on top. He modeled it after Italian designs, but he made so many changes that it was really his own design.

A French gentleman who was traveling through Virginia once came to Monticello after it was finished and he wrote to his friends in Europe describing Thomas Jefferson's house. "It resembles none of the others seen in this country," he said, "so that it may be said that Mr. Jefferson is the first American who has consulted the Fine Arts to know how he should shelter himself from the weather."

Monticello was not only beautiful; it was also an interesting place, full of new designs and inventions. Later, when Thomas had many important visitors, he designed a wall with shelves in the dining room that would swing open into the kitchen so that servants could serve him and his guests their dinner without listening to their private conversations.

Once Monticello was well under way, Thomas began to think more and more about a family. After all, no matter how beautiful a house might be, it wouldn't be very useful if there was no family to live in it. He was nearly thirty years old now. Most men married before then. Thomas's shyness had always made it hard for him to meet girls.

He still talked about such matters to his boyhood

friend Dabney Carr (who had married Thomas's sister Martha). "I'm the happiest man in the world, Thomas," Dabney told him. "You must find yourself a wife and know such happiness too."

Thomas agreed, but secretly he sometimes wondered if he would ever find the right person to marry.

Then one evening he met Martha Skelton at a party. She was a young woman, but she was already a widow. Her husband had died when she was only twenty years old. Thomas instantly fell in love with her, and he began to court her.

Today, we don't talk about "courting" anymore. Today people go on dates. But in earlier, more formal days, "dating" was a very serious business. You didn't just go to a girl's house and pick her up and take her to a dance. There were many rules to follow. When Thomas courted Martha, they both followed the rules.

Martha was a pretty young woman, with soft, light brown hair and large eyes that sparkled. Thomas thought they were the most wonderful things in the world, those shiny eyes that danced as he talked about poetry, music, and stately buildings.

He would come to her father's house, which was called The Forest, in a carriage. He was always careful to powder his hair and have his buckles shined. He would bow low when they met, and he *always* called her Mrs. Skelton.

"Good evening, Mrs. Skelton," he would say very formally.

"Good evening, Mr. Jefferson," Martha would reply

"Dating was a very serious business."

and she would curtsey. Her manners were flawless as she was a young woman from a prominent family. But Martha was more playful than Thomas and laughed when she called him Mr. Jefferson. She sometimes even teased him for being so solemn.

She was a lucky woman for her time—she had been to school, and had learned to dance and ride. But her greatest love was music. She was a fine harpsichord player. One of the reasons she and Thomas got along so well together was that they both loved music.

In fact, music helped Thomas in his courting. When he met Martha, there were two other men who also

45

wanted to marry her. They were both trying to impress her. Then one day, when they both came to her door at the same time, they heard music playing in the house. Martha was playing the harpsichord and Thomas was playing the violin. They looked through the window and saw the two gazing at each other as they played. They realized at once that Thomas and Martha were in love. So, they turned around and left, and never returned to Martha's house.

Finally, Thomas asked Martha to marry him, and she said yes. All at once, he realized with horror that he didn't have a house to bring a wife to. She asked him what was wrong. Thomas told her that Monticello wasn't finished yet. He didn't think it was right to bring a wife to only half a house.

When Martha heard why he was upset she laughed. "I don't mind an unfinished house!" she cried. "It will be fun to watch it grow."

So, on New Year's Day they were married at The Forest. The wedding was a big one, with fiddlers fiddling and servants serving and all the guests dancing. Dabney Carr, his bright eyes shining with happiness for his friend, smacked Thomas on the back and congratulated him on his beautiful bride. "So you have finally taken my advice, Thomas!" he said with a hearty laugh.

Then everyone watched as the bride and groom danced together in the center of the room. Thomas was nervous—his feet were so big he was afraid he'd trip Martha—but he was actually quite a good dancer. The old ladies nodded to each other and said what a lovely pair they made.

Afterwards, Thomas and Martha left in a carriage for their new home. As they left, it started to snow. After a few miles they had to leave the carriage behind and ride their horses through the thickly drifted roads. In the end they took a mountain path, and didn't get to Monticello until late at night.

When they arrived, the fires were out. The one finished room in the house was freezing cold. They were both shivering and tired. Their wedding clothes were ruined. Everything was so dismal they began to feel sad.

But then Thomas found a bottle of wine and lit a fire in the fireplace. He pulled out his violin. Soon the place was warm, and they were both singing and laughing. They were married after all and Thomas was happy. He wished that his sister Jane were alive to see his wife. He was sure that they would have been good friends.

"Come and meet your new daughter, Mr. Jefferson." Propped up in bed, Martha looked tired but happy. In her arms she held a tiny newborn baby. Thomas paused in the bedroom doorway. He couldn't speak.

He reached down and Martha put the baby in his arms. "She's perfect," he said in awe. "She's beautiful, just like her mother." Thomas could rarely recall such a joyful moment.

He insisted that they name the baby Martha after her mother. But they soon nicknamed her Patsy.

Thomas was very busy these days with work in the

"Thomas was very busy with work in the House of Burgesses."

House of Burgesses. He was a happy young man, working hard to understand the laws of Virginia, playing music with his wife, and watching his baby daughter grow. His best friend, Dabney Carr, was also doing well. He had just become a member of the House of Burgesses, and was already becoming famous.

Then one day in May, as Thomas was walking into the Assembly building, he heard terrible news. Dabney Carr had died while on business in Charlottesville. Thomas rushed into the building to find out if it was true. It was. His friend had gotten a fever while traveling, and the doctor wasn't able to cure it.

Thomas was heartbroken. He didn't know what to do. He felt helpless. Then, suddenly, he remembered a promise that he and Dabney had made when they were schoolboys—when one of them died, they had sworn, the other would bury him under the old oak tree on Little Mountain.

Thomas set out for home at once. When he got to Shadwell, he found that his sister Martha had buried her husband already. But it wasn't the right spot. Thomas had his friend's grave moved to just beneath the oak tree. Then he cleared the area around the tree by himself. Standing over the tombstone, he pictured Dabney's bright eyes, shining with life. He promised Dabney he would take care of his family. Sadly he bade his friend good-bye.

"You and the children must come to live with us now," he told his sister, "at Monticello." In time he became almost like a father to Dabney's six children.

But Thomas couldn't spend much time with his family these days. There was a new governor, Lord Dunmore, in Williamsburg. Unlike the old governor, who used to give parties for the members and ask their advice, Lord Dunmore was an arrogant man. He thought Virginia a wild and uncivilized place. He considered it beneath him to associate with the members of its Assembly. He decided that he did not need any help from the Virginians to govern the colony. Most of the time he found excuses to keep the Assembly from meeting.

Naturally, the members didn't like this one bit. The man was withholding their right to meet and make decisions about their own affairs. The members gathered in small groups and discussed the situation in low angry ns

he
ed
he
ad
ad
of
old
t.
rd
m.
the
nd
vas
wondering the same thing: would the other colonies join the fight?

CHAPTER SEVEN

Radical Steps

Four hundred miles away in Boston, strange things had happened. On the cold, clear night of December 16, 1773, packs of shadowy figures could be seen moving quietly from alley to alley. As they approached Boston Harbor their numbers grew. At the water's edge there finally stood what looked like hundreds of—Indians!

Men and boys from the city (and a few women) had disguised themselves as Indians. They now approached the creaking British ships that sat in the harbor. Silent as ghosts they crossed onto the docks and threw down planks to the ships.

Once they were on board, it was like a surprise party suddenly erupting.

"Here's what we think of your tea!" the men shouted as they hoisted the crates over their heads. With shrieks of delight, they thew them into the water.

"Have a cup, King George!"

"Don't choke on it!"

"Do you like it salty?"

They howled with laughter as they worked, cracking open the crates with tomahawks and spilling the tea leaves

Boston Tea Party.

over the water. Torches showed their faces gleaming with sweat, makeup, and delight.

When they were finished, the tea that had been sent all the way from England for Americans to buy lay ruined in the waters of the Harbor. Gleeful, but feeling suddenly frightened, the "Indians" hurried home. The Boston Tea Party was over.

But the consequences of the Party were soon to be felt. The British governor knew very well that no stray tribe of Indians had destroyed the British tea. He reacted at once.

First, he closed down Boston Harbor, so that the city could not receive or send supplies by water.

Next, he took the amazing step of abolishing all

forms of government in the colony of Massachusetts. The courts, the Assembly, even the sheriffs' offices were closed down. This shocked the colonists, for since they now had no local officials they were entirely at the mercy of the British.

They couldn't even discuss the matter, for the governor ruled that any political meeting was illegal. British soldiers marched through the streets of Boston, making sure no meetings were held. The people watched from their doorways and wondered what they could do.

In Williamsburg, the rider now gave his message to the Virginians. The British were treating the colonists of Massachusetts like criminals and the colony needed their support. He asked the members of the Assembly to meet with the leaders of all the other colonies in one great assembly, a Congress.

The members began to discuss what they could do. "The colonies must support each other," some said, "or the same thing will happen to us all."

Many of the men were unsure and thought it best to bide their time. But the other members weren't content to wait. They wanted to find a way to show their support for the people of Massachusetts. This was a serious business—the most serious in the history of the colony. Some younger members, including Patrick Henry, Richard Henry Lee, and Thomas Jefferson, decided to have their own meeting outside the Assembly. They went to a pub in Williamsburg called the Raleigh Tavern to discuss what they should do.

"They went to a pub in Williamsburg called the Raleigh Tavern."

"Why don't we write a paper to the King? We will tell him that Virginia protests the actions of the British in Massachusetts!" one said. Many members liked this idea.

Then Thomas Jefferson asked to speak. He said that it might be better to do something that would really show the people of Virginia how serious the matter was. After all, he said, it was extremely important that all Virginians know what was going on.

"Good idea!" cried Richard Henry Lee, a fiery young radical.

"But what can we do?" someone asked.

Thomas Jefferson looked around the room. He smiled. "We can be quiet," he said.

"What is that supposed to mean?" asked Patrick Henry, who never liked being quiet.

Thomas then explained that if they announced a day of fasting and prayer in Virginia—an entire day in which all the colonists would not eat and would pray for Massachusetts—it would give the people time to think about how serious the situation was.

The other members loved the idea. Everyone congratulated young Thomas Jefferson. Patrick Henry clapped him on the back and said that Thomas Jefferson was not only a great thinker, but a great *American* thinker.

Rising quickly from the table, they all marched back to the House of Burgesses. They put Thomas's plan before the entire Assembly, asking them to vote on it—yes or no. Every single member voted "yes."

The plan worked beautifully. For a whole day, all across Virginia nobody worked or played or went to market. And while the people sat at home fasting and praying, they had time to think about what England was doing to them. The more they thought about it, the less they liked it.

When Lord Dunmore, usually so cool and official, heard about these goings-on, he reacted with rage. *How dare the Virginians support those upstarts from Massachusetts?* He would put a stop to their rebellious actions at once.

Following the example of the Massachusetts governor, he issued a proclamation from his mansion: from that moment on, the Virginia House of Burgesses was to be closed for good.

Red-coated soldiers marched down the wide central street in Williamsburg and came to a halt in front of the Assembly building. A worried throng of townspeople watched as they wrapped a heavy chain around the door-handles and clamped it with a lock.

This infuriated the members, even the older, more conservative ones. Nearly all of them now marched across to the Raleigh Tavern. There, on an afternoon in August 1774, they formed their own House of Burgesses. Their first decision was to send a delegation to the Congress in Philadelphia.

When the first Continental Congress met in Philadelphia in September, all of the most important Virginia delegates attended. But Thomas Jefferson was not there. He was still a very young man, after all, and older members were chosen first. But he was full of ideas and plans, and at home in Monticello, he eagerly awaited news from the Virginia delegation. Despite the grave situation, he felt he was the luckiest man in the world. All the ideas he had been carried away by as a student were suddenly being acted out right before him.

Filled with enthusiasm, Thomas started to write out his own thoughts about the rights of Americans. Knowing he couldn't be with the delegates who were going to Philadelphia, he finished the paper and gave it to them to read at the Continental Congress.

Many of them thought Thomas's paper was too

strong. They knew it would anger the British and didn't dare support it officially. But some of Thomas Jefferson's friends were so impressed by its force and truth that they managed to have it printed privately. They called it "A Summary View of the Rights of British Americans."

First people in Williamsburg read it, then people in Philadelphia. Soon people all over the colonies were secretly passing around copies of Thomas Jefferson's paper, reading with growing excitement what it said about the rights not only of Americans but all peoples. In time, it became popular even in England.

Without even knowing it, Thomas Jefferson was becoming a famous writer!

Next, near the end of 1774, Governor Dunmore closed down the courts in Virginia. Thomas Jefferson later joked that this put him out of a job. Although he didn't know it then, he would never practice law again. From now on there would always be more important things to do.

The members of the new House of Burgesses, who now called themselves the Convention of Virginia, met again in March 1775. Because they were afraid that the governor might try to stop them, they met in Richmond instead of Williamsburg. Today Richmond is a big city, the capital of Virginia, but then it was little more than a village. There wasn't even a hall big enough for the Assembly to meet in. Instead the meeting was held in a church called St. John's.

The Assembly had to make a decision. What should they do next? Should they try to talk to King George once more? Some people said that wouldn't do any good—the king had never listened to them, and there was no reason to think he would listen now. The members argued back and forth. Some urged caution, others wanted immediate action to show the mother country that the colonies were very unhappy.

Then Patrick Henry rose to his feet.

His voice was impassioned. Why were the members so slow to see the truth? "England is not the mother country," he cried, "but the enemy!" He stood before them, straight as an arrow, his eyes wild with excitement. "Gentlemen," he said, "I propose that Virginia be put into a state of defense! We must be ready for war!"

The older members of the Convention gaped at him. Fight? "It would be crazy to fight England!" they said. "England is the most powerful country in the world!"

Next, Richard Henry Lee, who was also a great speaker, strode to the front and stood beside Patrick Henry.

"Gentlemen," he cried, his high voice pitched almost as in a song, "I declare to you that this is the only course open to us. We must be prepared for war, because war will surely come."

At that point, Thomas Jefferson stood up. Everyone stared at him. He was not only very young, but he almost never spoke at meetings. He took notes and wrote papers, but he was usually too shy to actually speak. Now, though, he knew it was time. He walked up and stood beside Patrick Henry and Richard Henry Lee. He was so nervous his legs were shaking, but his voice rang out confidently.

"I must agree with my colleagues," he said. "A careful view of the situation before us will reveal that we have no other choice. England has never treated her colonies fairly, and she never will. If we believe in our rights, we must prepare to fight!"

Patrick Henry suddenly raised his arms. His hands were shaking and the muscles in his neck stood out. He spoke loudly, his voice ringing through the church. The members all leaned forward, half frightened, but listening intently. Even the ones who were most opposed to war were slowly rising to their feet.

"There is no longer any room for hope!" Patrick Henry thundered, his voice ringing clear as a bell. "We must fight! I repeat, sir, we must fight! Gentlemen may cry 'peace, peace'—but there is no peace. The war has actually begun."

He looked around at his fellow Virginians, his eyes flashing. Then he finished:

"I know not what course others may take—but as for me . . . give me liberty, or give me death!"

When he sat down, the only sound in the church was of the wind blowing through the open windows. Outside they could hear children playing and birds calling, but inside all was still and tense. The men sat thinking about Patrick Henry's words. Finally, Richard Henry Lee spoke again, calmly now, and formally supported Patrick Henry's motion.

The Assembly voted to fight. It was a close vote:

sixty-five to sixty, once they had made the decision they knew there was no turning back.

Thomas's head was spinning. There was so much to do, so many plans to make.

The Convention worked furiously now. They elected a group of men to see to it that the colony was armed. Thomas Jefferson was one of them. His job was to make sure the men of Virginia had rifles and toma-hawks, and, last but not least, that they had the official uniform of the Revolutionary soldiers—a hunting shirt. Soon, men all over Virginia were printing the words "LIBERTY OR DEATH" on their hunting shirts. And within no time, even young children knew the words of Patrick Henry's speech.

CHAPTER EIGHT

The First Shots

On the chilly night of April 18, 1775, a fleet of boats paddled silently across Boston Harbor. In the boats were several hundred British troops. Their leader was Lt. Colonel Francis Smith. He had orders to march to the small town of Concord, sixteen miles away, and destroy all the muskets and gunpowder the colonists had stored there. In Massachusetts, as in Virginia, men were preparing for war.

The British wanted to work at night, secretly, so that they could avoid fighting openly with the patriots. They hoped that by destroying these supplies they would make the Americans lose heart.

What Lt. Colonel Smith did not know was that American spies were everywhere, swarming in the woods, hiding behind rocks and trees, watching the approach of the British.

A man was dispatched on horseback to warn the patriots. His name was Paul Revere. He reached the town of Lexington, between Boston and Concord, before the troops even started marching. There he warned Samuel Adams and John Hancock, two leaders of the Massachusetts patriots, and the townspeople.

When the soldiers reached the village of Lexington,

the gray light of early dawn revealed a surprising sight. A band of about seventy patriots stood before them on the village green, with muskets in their hands, and grim, determined looks on their faces.

John Pitcairn, second in command of the British forces, rode forward on his horse. Surveying the ragged lines of patriots, he laughed loudly, asked what they thought they were doing, and told them to throw down their muskets and flee for their lives.

Captain Jonas Parker, leader of the patriot forces, refused to give ground.

Lt. Colonel Smith gave a sharp order, and the smart lines of British soldiers began forming a circle to surround the patriots. At that, the Americans began to retreat slowly toward the village, keeping their guns aimed at the redcoats. There was a long, tense pause, where neither side knew what would happen.

Suddenly a shot rang out. No one knew whether an American or a British soldier fired first, but at the sound, the muskets of the mighty British forces opened fire. The patriots, mostly farmers, fled in retreat, firing the occasional shot as they ran.

Lt. Colonel Smith was greatly pleased with this easy victory. His men gave a great shout and advanced toward their destination, Concord.

However, the patriots were not finished. All through the night they had been swarming from the surrounding villages to the defense of Concord. By early afternoon, when the British reached the North Bridge in Concord,

"British forces open fire."

four hundred farmers, blacksmiths, cobblers, and carpenters were waiting for them on the other side.

A short, vicious battle took place, muskets blazing on both sides. At last, the British, realizing that their plan of a sneak attack on the armory had failed, withdrew from the town.

But the patriots weren't satisfied. These soldiers from a land three thousand miles away had marched deep into their lands, intending to take what was theirs, to steal the guns and supplies they needed to protect themselves. Hundreds more farmers from all the villages in the area swept down onto the road. They took up positions behind trees and rocks, behind barns and stone walls, and, taking careful aim, fired on the British.

Many British soldiers died right there, but Lt. Col. Smith was a clever leader. He sent parties out into the woods to circle back around the patriots. These parties killed dozens of patriots by sneaking up on them from the rear.

By the time the British made their way back to Lexington, they found a force of twelve hundred more redcoats waiting to reinforce them. This enormous army now made a stately procession back toward Boston.

Still the New England farmers continued to attack. Hour after hour they ducked into positions behind trees, and took aim at the invaders. The fighting continued until nightfall when the British reached the safety of Charleston Harbor.

On that day, April 19, 1775, 273 British soldiers and 95 American patriots died. Over a year before America's leaders officially declared independence, the farmers of Massachusetts showed their support for the cause of freedom.

On the very next night, hundreds of miles to the south, the Virginians got a chance to show their support as well. Governor Dunmore had heard about how the colonists were preparing to fight. He too sent soldiers to take their gunpowder, which was stored in Williamsburg.

The farmers of Virginia were furious. Patrick Henry, who always liked to move swiftly, decided this was the

"The fighting continued."

perfect time for action. On his own, he gathered a group
of soldiers made up of men and boys from local farms,
and led them on a march into Williamsburg. Thomas
Jefferson's young brother, Randolph, was one of these
soldiers.

Gathering in force outside the Governor's Palace,
these proud men, forced the governor to pay for the powder without bloodshed. The governor paid up, but he
didn't like it. He proclaimed Patrick Henry a dangerous
outlaw, hoping to frighten the people. But this idea backfired—now the Virginia colonists started calling Patrick
Henry a hero.

CHAPTER NINE

A Roomful of Revolutionaries

A few weeks after the Battle of Lexington and Concord, Thomas Jefferson got some surprising news. Peyton Randolph, the leader of the Virginia delegates in Philadelphia, had been called back to Williamsburg. Thomas Jefferson was the alternate. This meant that he had to go to Philadelphia as Randolph's replacement. He was now an official member of the Virginia delegation to the Congress.

When Thomas first entered the grand corridors of the State House in Philadelphia he was greeted by a roomful of new faces. He knew all the members from Virginia, especially Richard Henry Lee and big, happy Benjamin Harrison, who were standing together talking when he walked in. The new commander of the Continental army, George Washington—who had been a military leader since the French and Indian War back in 1754—was across the room.

But now Thomas met John Adams for the first time. Mr. Adams was a delegate from Massachusetts. He was a short man, rather plump, with a sharp tongue and sharp, lively eyes. He and Thomas took to each other right away. Thomas was nervous at first because Adams was famous throughout the colonies. He had been one of the first men to argue that America had to revolt against her rulers.

"This is a great honor, Mr. Adams," Thomas stammered.

John Adams surprised Thomas by saying that he was very pleased to meet the famous Mr. Jefferson. He had been impressed by Mr. Jefferson's paper on American rights.

"A most handsome public paper," he said. "Mr. Jefferson, you have a masterly pen."

Thomas also met other men: Samuel Chase from Maryland, Caesar Rodney from Delaware, John Dickinson from Pennsylvania, and John Jay from New York.

Most of these men were older than Thomas, but John Jay was about his age. He was a short man with a broad forehead and piercing eyes that shone with intelligence. Thomas talked to him about his visit to New York, and Jay asked questions about Virginia. They had no idea as they stood chatting about each other's colony that one of them would become president of the United States, and the other would become the first chief justice of the Supreme Court.

But there was one man Thomas was more eager to meet than all the others. He was an old man, but he was still very active. He was probably the most famous man in America because of the many things he had been: in-

Franklin, Washington, Adams.

ventor, printer, scientist, and now member of Congress from Pennsylvania. His name was Benjamin Franklin.

Franklin was bald on top but had long, flowing gray hair at the sides and back that rested on his shoulders. His face was old and sagging, but his eyes were as lively as a boy's.

Jefferson and Franklin were both very formal when they were introduced, as was the custom of the time. Thomas said, "Dr. Franklin," and bowed. And Benjamin Franklin said, "Mr. Jefferson," and he bowed too.

But in a short time Dr. Franklin realized that this young Virginian was a genuine thinker. Soon they were tripping over their words, covering all sorts of topics. Thomas was thrilled by all the things the famous man had accomplished. Dr. Franklin described the public library he had started and told Thomas about the public fire department he had organized in Philadelphia. His mind jumped quickly from subject to subject. Recently, he said, he had seen a hot air balloon. Perhaps it could be used to deliver mail quickly—the first airmail! Thomas laughed.

Encouraged by Dr. Franklin's lively mind, Thomas told him about an idea he had to change the currency in America. At that time each of the colonies printed its own money. There were pounds, shillings, dollars, guineas, and pistareens. It was all terribly confusing. How much simpler it would be, Thomas observed, if all the colonies used the same money.

"Why, that's a marvelous idea!" Dr. Franklin exclaimed. "I hope that when our work is finished here we shall be able to act upon it."

It was the most fascinating conversation Thomas Jefferson had ever had. That night, when he went back to the guesthouse where he was staying, he was too excited to sleep. He lay in bed, staring at the ceiling. Ben Franklin's full life was proof to him that ideas could be made useful. He lay awake and thought about all the things he hoped to accomplish in the future.

All through the hot summer of 1775 Thomas worked with the Congress. There were meetings every day. The members sat in the stuffy State House and listened to speeches about tax problems, army problems, legal problems. Thomas didn't speak much, but he paid close attention and took notes of everything he thought was important. John Adams, on the other hand, who had become a close friend, was always jumping up shouting "Mr. President! Mr. President!" to get the attention of John Hancock, the president of the Congress.

Through the autumn of 1775 and into 1776 the delegates worked at the difficult task of putting together an army. The Congress decided each man in the army would be given one pound of beef, one pound of bread, and one pound of potatoes for rations every day. They also bought cannons and gunpowder, and even hired soldiers all the way from Ireland.

Thomas had been given a special task. He was to try and convince the people of Canada to join the Americans in fighting the British. He wrote that "the delegates of Canada will join us in Congress, and complete the American union." As we know today, Thomas Jefferson was wrong about this!

In December of 1775 news came to Philadelphia that Governor Dunmore of Virginia was causing trouble once more. He was raiding plantations, the reports said, trying to root out the conspirators who were causing so much trouble for England.

Thomas suddenly became worried about his family's safety. He hadn't heard from his wife for some time. "The suspense under which I am is too terrible to be endured," he wrote to a friend. Finally Martha wrote to say that the family was well, but Thomas was still concerned. He canceled his meetings and left town for Virginia.

He entered his home colony feeling tired and worried. Still, when he turned a bend in the road and saw the hills that he knew so well he suddenly felt happy and calm. Monticello looked beautiful. The fruit trees were healthy, the peas were ripening in the pea patch, and the house was finally starting to look like his finished drawings.

But when he reached the house Martha greeted him in a troubled voice. His mother had been very ill, she told him.

When Thomas was taken to see his mother, he was shocked. She didn't look like the same woman. Her face was shrunken and wrinkled, her hands shook as she embraced him. She was fifty-seven years old now, and she had been getting steadily weaker over the past few years. Thomas wanted to be near her, so he stayed home longer than he had planned. In March of 1776, his mother died.

The events of the past year caught up with him now. He became sick and depressed. Both of his parents were dead, as well as his older sister Jane. He couldn't help feeling that death was always present, in the midst of all his activity. He suddenly wondered why he bothered doing anything, when eventually he and everyone he knew would be dead.

In his whole life Thomas was only sick a few times. But now he developed a migraine headache of such intensity that he had to stay in bed for days on end. All he could do was lie on his back, tossing from side to side and brooding over how sad everything was. So many people he loved had died. There was so much pain in life, so much fighting.

He even started to wonder about his work. England was such a powerful country, it was insane to fight a war.

71

Many young American men would surely die. Mothers would lose their sons. America would become weaker, not stronger. Maybe it was better to just go on living under British rule.

For five weeks he lay in bed, feeling miserable and worrying about his family. At any moment British troops might come rushing into Monticello. There was so much to do, but he was so tired, so tired of it all.

Then, suddenly, everything changed. A friend sent him a booklet written by an Englishman named Thomas Paine who had come to America because he believed in the cause of American independence. The booklet was called "Common Sense." In it, Tom Paine argued in strong, clear language that the Americans had a right to fight the British.

Paine thought the colonists, living far from the British Isles, had the idea that a king was such a special, mysterious person—almost godlike—that it would be unthinkable to rebel against him.

But in "Common Sense" Paine proclaimed that the noblemen of England were nothing but "rascals" who had made themselves powerful by taking away the people's rights. A good government, he said, was one in which the people decided matters for themselves.

Thomas nodded as he read. These were ideas that he had always believed in. And here they were, expressed by an Englishman!

He read further, his excitement growing. Tom Paine wrote: "Of more worth is an honest man to society, and in the sight of God, than all the crowned ruffians that ever lived."

Thomas Jefferson, sitting up now in bed, nodded vigorously. Yes, he thought, this was true! Without noticing what he was doing, he got up, and began pacing back and forth across the room.

The English kings had caused too much pain and bloodshed, Tom Paine went on. They must be stopped. "O ye that love mankind! ye that dare oppose not only the tyranny but the tyrant, stand forth!"

Thomas was flinging clothes around the room now, hurriedly getting dressed. Of course! Of course Tom Paine was right! It was what he himself had believed all along—that rights were not something vague, but something real, something to fight for.

Martha ran into the room and saw him struggling with a boot.

"What are you doing?" she asked.

He told her he had to go at once, there was work to be done.

"What about your headache?"

He stopped and looked at her. He smiled. It was gone.

He called for horses to be made ready, and a coach. Why was he lying around in bed? He was needed in Philadelphia! There was work for him to do. There were plans to be made. There were rights to fight for!

CHAPTER TEN

The Course of Human Events

On June 7, 1776, Richard Henry Lee stood up to make a speech to his fellow delegates in the State House in Philadelphia. Proudly he declared that the Virginia members were ready to vote for independence. He moved that the Congress prepare a Declaration of Independence. John Adams leaped to his feet and seconded the motion. Months of meeting and fighting, debate and discussion had finally come down to this decision. The delegates cheered and called for a vote.

But there was a problem. Some of the delegates didn't know if the people of their colonies were ready to separate from England, yet. John Dickinson of Pennsylvania said he would like the Congress to wait while messengers were sent to find out. The Congress agreed to this, and messengers were sent.

In the meantime, they chose five men to plan and write the document announcing their decision—the Declaration of Independence. Thomas Jefferson, John Adams, and Benjamin Franklin were in the group.

So now we are back to the beginning of this story.

The other delegates voted to have Adams and Jefferson decide between them who the writer should be. John Adams and Thomas Jefferson argued about it, and, as you know, Jefferson finally agreed to write the Declaration.

The next morning Thomas prepared to work. He set up his specially made portable writing desk, which he always carried with him. It looked like a book when it was shut, but the top opened up to form a desk top. Inside was a drawer where he kept pens, ink, and sand. The pens were made of goose feathers. People wrote by dipping the tips into the ink. Since the ink took a long time to dry, they had to sprinkle sand onto the page when they were done so that the sand would absorb the extra ink.

Thomas liked to write standing up. He said he could think better that way. So he stood up at the little desk, set up the pens and ink and put the little box of sand beside him. Then he took a sheet of paper and smoothed it out on the desk.

He felt good this morning. He knew what he wanted to write and he felt that he could do it. Standing near the window, he noticed that there was a crack in the wall right by the window. He thought it looked like the shape of the Virginia border, which his father had helped to make. He thought back to the stories his father used to tell about his adventures exploring the wilderness. He was having an adventure of his own now. In fact, the whole country was.

He dipped his pen into the ink and began to write.

Some time later he stopped and read what he had

"Thomas liked to write standing up."

written, then took some sand from the box and sprinkled it over the sheet. He let it stand for a moment, then blew it off.

So far, so good. He liked it. The Declaration ought to be strong, but it also ought to be persuasive and beautiful. The language should inspire people. Thomas wanted it to be more than just a legal document that would be filed in a book and forgotten. He wanted to create something that people would remember for a long time. And not just Americans—it should be written for all people.

So he began by saying that what was happening in America could happen anywhere, depending on the situation.

Thomas Jefferson wrote:

"When in the course of human events it becomes necessary for a people to dissolve the political bands which have connected them with another . . . they should declare the causes which impel them to the separation."

When he said "in the course of human events," he meant that such things can happen to other people at other times, that America was not the only place where people could declare their freedom. It just so happened that "the course of human events" had led the Americans to be first.

In the last part of the sentence he used the word "impel," which means "force": "they should declare the causes which impel them to the separation." Here he was saying that England had forced the Americans to separate.

It was important that the world understand that the Americans were not doing this simply because they wanted to, but because they had no choice.

America had to separate because the rights of its people were not guaranteed. These were basic human rights that all people were entitled to:

"We hold these truths to be self-evident: that all men are created equal; that they are endowed by their creator with certain unalienable rights; that among these are life, liberty, and the pursuit of happiness."

This was what Thomas Jefferson believed more strongly than anything else—that all people were equal and nobody should be treated better than anybody else. There were some rights that could not be taken away. Of course, every person had the right to be alive. A person also had the right to liberty—to be free to think and do what he wants, as long as his actions do not reduce the liberty of someone else. Finally, people had a right to be happy and to do what makes them happy.

There was only one way to protect these rights. The government must get its power from the people, not the other way around. The next sentence Thomas wrote stated this.

"That, to secure these rights, governments are instituted among men, deriving their just powers from the consent of the governed."

Thomas Jefferson stated that the Americans intended not only to become free of England, but to set up a government in which the people would be in charge.

"He left his room and went outside into the street."

He smiled. It was going well. He sanded the page, then put it away. He left his room and went outside into the street.

It was evening. Horses clopped along the cobblestone street. Two boys walked past arm in arm. They were singing a song that children often sung:

Our King the Good
No Man of Blood.
The Lion bold
The Lamb doth hold.
The Moon gives Light
In Time of Night.

Nightingales sing
In Time of Spring.

It was an old song. Thomas smiled at the first part—"Our King the Good." That song would soon change, he thought.

CHAPTER ELEVEN

Scientists in the Lab

I nside Smith's Tavern, a lively spot in downtown Philadelphia where Thomas usually went for dinner, he met his friends John Adams and Benjamin Harrison. He often saw Harrison here, as this was where the Virginia members of Congress usually met, but he was surprised to see John Adams sitting beside him.

Adams said he had come to talk with the Virginia delegates about the vote for independence. He was nervous about it. Some of the members from the middle states—Pennsylvania, New York, New Jersey, Maryland, and Delaware—might not agree, he said. He sat beating his fists on the wooden table nervously.

Benjamin Harrison was smiling and eating a big steak.

"There's nothing to worry about!" he told Adams. "All the delegates will agree to the Declaration of Independence. Especially, I'm sure, when they see the moving and melodious words of my fellow Virginian."

He smiled broadly at Thomas.

"I hope the words will live up to your praise,"

Thomas said. "And I agree that the members from Pennsylvania and the other middle states will vote for independence, but I think it is important to let them take their time. If only the New England and Southern colonies agree, America will fail. The two ends need the middle."

Just then the door opened and to their surprise Benjamin Franklin walked in. As Franklin had been ill recently, he stayed at home as much as possible. He greeted them and sat down, saying that he was feeling a little better and wanted to get out a bit in the warm summer air.

The men fell to talking about England's policy of taxing the colonies without allowing them representation in Parliament. John Adams flared up and started listing all the injustices that King George had committed in America. Ben Harrison said the king was obviously a madman.

But Ben Franklin had a different view of things. He was older and wiser than the other delegates to the Congress and had spent many years in England. Naturally, everyone listened to him.

"In a way," he began, "it isn't the king's fault. History is changing, my friends. Ideas are changing. King George simply has old ideas. That, I believe, is the real problem."

John Adams pounded the table with his fist and said that that was what gave the Americans the right to be free.

Franklin agreed. He went on to say that the Americans were trying to do something that had never been done before. They were trying to build a brand new country, based on new ideas. Founding a country, Ben Franklin said, was like being a scientist working in a lab. You were trying to make something new, and while you might have a pretty good idea what it would be like, you couldn't be sure it would work. You just had to try your hardest and hope for the best.

Thomas Jefferson interrupted to say that the ideas they were using were new, but they hadn't been the first to think of them. European philosophers had been developing ideas about fair governments for some time.

One of these philosophers was John Locke, an Englishman who had lived about a hundred years before the American Revolution. All of the American patriot leaders had read Locke's books about government. Thomas Jefferson in particular was influenced by Locke's ideas.

Locke wrote that all men have a natural right "to order and dispose of their possessions and persons as they think fit, within the bounds of nature, without asking leave, or depending upon the will of any other man." Thomas had learned this from Dr. Small and he believed it now as strongly as ever.

Locke also said that if the government withheld these rights, the people were entitled to revolt. He said that if the leaders ruled by "a long train of abuses," then the people should "rouse themselves, and endeavor to put the rule into such hands which may secure to them the ends for which government was first erected."

So Jefferson was right in saying that the idea of revolution was not new with the American patriots.

Many other men besides Locke had influenced them as well. The works of Sir Isaac Newton, the famous scientist, were very popular among the American leaders. Even though Newton was a scientist, his ideas helped to change the way people thought about government. He had used his reason to discover basic forces in the world, like gravity. He did it by observing and asking questions (like why apples fall down).

After Newton, other people began to use reason to explore non-scientific things. Locke asked questions about government that people had never thought to ask before, like:

Why should we have a king? Why should we serve him? What does our government do for us?

Locke decided that the only reason for having a government was so that it could help the people. The government should serve the people, Locke thought. Everyone had been thinking backwards, that the people should serve the government, the king.

So now Jefferson, Franklin, Adams, and the other leaders had decided that America should form its own government, and that this government must serve the people. This great idea came from the European thinkers. It was the Americans who would put it to the test.

"And the first step," Ben Franklin told his friends, "is to make a proper Declaration—to state the principles that Americans believe in."

Thomas Jefferson nodded and said that was what he hoped he had done.

"And," John Adams said, "the Declaration must also

list the things England has done to force America to break away."

"That," said Thomas, "is what I hope to do next."

Back in his room, Thomas began making a list. He listed in the Declaration of Independence all of the rights of Americans that the King had violated. There were so many of them that when you read it the repeated words "he has" sound like a bell ringing:

He has forbidden his governors to pass laws of immediate and pressing importance . . .

He has dissolved representative houses repeatedly . . .

He has obstructed the administration of justice . . .

He has made judges dependent on his will alone . . .

He has erected a multitude of new offices, and sent hither swarms of officers to harass our people, and eat out their substance.

He has plundered our seas, ravaged our coasts, burnt our towns, and destroyed the lives of our people.

It was a harsh list, but the truth was harsh. He was stating the case for America. It had to be powerful.

When he finished, he put down his pen and relaxed, breathing in the night air. He thought about what Ben Franklin had said, that founding a country was like being a scientist in a lab. The members of the Congress were scientists. Their first experiment was about to begin. He hoped it would work.

CHAPTER TWELVE

Choosing Freedom

When Thomas finished the Declaration, he took it to Adams and Franklin to look over. They were both very pleased with it. Then it went before the whole Congress. Most people liked it, but still there was some debate. They wanted to change some of the wording, and several members objected to one point or another.

While everyone discussed changing what he had written, Thomas sat squirming in his seat. Benjamin Franklin looked over at him and chuckled. He said Thomas looked awfully uncomfortable. The chairs were too small, Thomas told him. His big legs were sticking out.

Franklin smiled broadly. He knew the real reason for all the squirming. He understood what it was like to have to listen to other people talking about what you had done. He told Thomas a story.

When Ben Franklin was a young man and still working as a printer, he had a friend who was opening a hat shop. The friend had made a sign for the shop which said: "JOHN THOMPSON, HATTER, MAKES AND SELLS HATS FOR

READY MONEY." On the bottom was a picture of a hat. Franklin's friend liked the sign very much, and he showed it to his friends to see what they thought.

The first friend said that he didn't need to say "hatter" because he also said "makes hats." So he took out the word. The next friend said he didn't need to say "makes" because nobody cared that he made the hats, only that he sold them. So now the sign said: "John Thompson sells hats for ready money."

Then a third friend said that he didn't need to say "for ready money" because everyone knows that you sell things for money. So, he took that out too. Now the sign just said: "John Thompson sells hats."

The poor hatter thought that his friends were finally finished making changes to his sign, but he was wrong. A fourth friend said he didn't need to say "sells hats" because there was a picture of a hat. So, he took that out too.

Thus, he ended up with a sign that just said his name, "John Thompson," and had a picture of a hat.

Thomas laughed at the story. It made him feel better, but he still didn't like everyone talking about changing the Declaration.

In the end, only a few changes were made, and they were mostly small ones. But there was one big change, and Thomas was angry about it.

When Thomas was in the Virginia House of Burgesses he had tried to pass a law about slavery. When it didn't pass he promised himself he would try again someday. Now in the Declaration of Independence he had added a part which accused the British of bringing the slaves to America against the wishes of the Americans. He was hoping that someday when America was an independent country this passage might be used to help free the slaves.

But it didn't work. Many members of Congress owned slaves, and many people in America still thought they needed slaves to run their plantations, especially in the South. So the Congress took out the part about slavery. Besides, they said, it wasn't really the king's fault that there was slavery. And they were right: slavery really was the fault of the American people.

At last, on July 4, 1776, the Congress agreed to the Declaration of Independence. On July 8, it was read in the street outside the State House, and a crowd of people gathered and cheered until they were hoarse. A contingent of soldiers, decked out in the new uniforms of the American army, shot off their muskets in salute.

All the bells in all the churches in Philadelphia rang, and they kept ringing all day and all night. America had declared itself free, and the people celebrated for the first time—not on the 4th of July, this time, but on the 8th.

While people shook hands and shouted, Thomas Jefferson stood quietly within the shadow of the State House. He smiled, proud of the work they had done. But he knew that it was just a beginning. Soon terrible work would start: the work of war.

War and Pain

The fighting started almost immediately. In August of 1776, General George Washington found himself in command of American soldiers in New York City, trying desperately to stop a British invasion. The Americans were outnumbered, and the rough, undertrained young men watched in terror as smart British troops marched in crisp, even lines toward their positions. Also in the British army were several thousand Hessians, tough German soldiers hired by England to fight the American rebels.

Within a week the more disciplined British troops drove the patriots first into a desperate retreat onto the island of Manhattan, then up into Harlem, and finally out of the city. Not satisfied with the capture of one of America's most important cities, the British commander continued chasing the scared and defeated patriot army into New Jersey.

During the months before independence was proclaimed, many Americans had warned that the British army was too powerful for the rebels. Now the worn, bedraggled farmers and merchants of the American battalions were learning the truth of that opinion.

In late November, the English general, Lord Cornwallis, decided to stop the chase and rest for the winter. George Washington's exhausted army rested on the banks of the Delaware River. They felt lucky to have a break. They had lost hundreds of men, and many others had deserted, frightened by the terrifying approach of the British troops. Of those who were left, many were wounded and all were tired, hungry, and badly in need of rest.

At this moment George Washington showed his tactical genius. An attack was the last thing the British leaders would expect from the tired American forces, so that's just what he would do.

Quickly, he sent orders for reinforcements from the North. Gathering these and his own men across the river from the British-held town of Trenton, he planned his strategy. His exhausted men complained that it was impossible for them to go on. Why not wait for spring? By then the army would be strong again.

Washington refused to listen. Instead, he read them the words of a great writer—an Englishman—who understood what they were fighting for. Sitting around camp fires in the cold December darkness, their eyes gleaming, the men listened:

"These are times that try men's souls. The summer soldier and the sunshine patriot will, in this crisis, shrink from the service of their country; but he that stands it now, deserves the love and thanks of man and woman."

Tom Paine had done it again. He had once more

captured in writing the needs of the moment. And the men of Washington's army responded. They remembered all they were fighting for and, strength returning to their tired limbs, they swore to follow Washington wherever he would lead.

So then, on Christmas night, Washington ordered 2,800 men into boats. The freezing winds, the darkness, and the huge ice chunks floating downriver made the crossing next to impossible. Washington pushed on and, against all odds, the army made it to the opposite shore.

There, as the cold sun climbed over the snowy horizon, Washington formed his ragged men into two lines and marched into the city. The patriots found the British and Hessian soldiers still smug from victory and sleepy from their Christmas celebrations. Sweeping through the streets, General Washington and his patriot army swiftly routed the enemy and took control of the town.

So the first painful year of war ended hopefully. The Americans had won a surprising victory at the Battle of Trenton. But it was hard fought, and many long years of struggle were to follow.

Hundreds of miles to the south, Thomas Jefferson, one of Virginia's most famous citizens, had become the state's governor. The war hadn't yet reached the South, but reminders of the fighting were all around. Towns and people had become poor, their money gone to support the soldiers. Once busy marketplaces were deserted. With so many men gone off to war, fields lay fallow. Nearly every family had had a son, father, uncle, or cousin killed or captured by the British and on every street were houses draped in the black cloth of mourning.

The people of Virginia knew the war was coming; they were afraid, and they needed a strong leader. Thomas Jefferson, however, was no soldier. He did not have the leadership ability of George Washington. He was a thinker, and his strongest belief was that democracy would win in the end. A strong leader was a threat to the people, he believed.

But during war a strong leader is necessary. So, while Thomas held to his deeply felt beliefs, they were to cause him and his state much pain.

Most of the war had taken place in the North so far. But late in 1778, the British, surprised and dismayed at their recent losses, decided to move south. They traveled by sea, bypassing Virginia, and landed forces in South Carolina and Georgia.

They had better luck in the South. By late 1779, the British had won a string of victories. There were rumors that they would march on Virginia. Virginia had almost no guns or powder, but Thomas made a decision to send what supplies he could to aid the army in South Carolina in an effort to stop the British there. Even the horses and wagons at Monticello were sent.

It helped a little, but it wasn't long before the steadily advancing British line reached Virginia. Thomas sent a young friend of his, James Monroe, to keep lookout for their approach on Richmond, which was now the state capital. One afternoon a soldier dashed into Governor

Jefferson's office with a message from James Monroe that the British army was now heading straight for Richmond.

Thomas Jefferson, calm as ever, nodded. He gave the man orders to gather some of his important papers. Then he went to the window and looked out with his special spyglass. He sat down and held his head in his hands, thinking. Why was this happening? Should he have kept a greater force to guard the boarders? What had he done wrong?

There was no time to think. Soon the British soldiers appeared, marching through the streets in their red uniforms. They wheeled three cannons into the town and fired them. One cannonball blew a hole in the roof of the butcher's house. The butcher's wife and children ran out into the street, screaming. Everyone in town fled.

Thomas leaped onto his horse and escaped just in time. He made for a nearby town where he hoped to find General von Steuben, a German in command of a contingent of American forces, but when he got there he found the general had gone. Not stopping to rest, he rode on, pounding along the dusty roads, wondering all the while what he had allowed to happen to Virginia. For three days and nights he continued, stopping only to give orders. He rode so hard that his horse died of exhaustion right on the road.

Desperate to stop the ruin he felt he had brought to his state, Thomas worked in a frenzy, rounding up scattered troops and trying to find fresh supplies. His efforts were too late. The British stormed through Virginia, taking what they wanted.

Soon after the British invasion, Jefferson's term as governor ended. His friends, who knew that despite his failures as governor he was still one of the great leaders of the Revolution, wanted him to run again. Thomas firmly refused. He had let Virginia down. Many people were angry with him, and he could not blame them. Some said he shouldn't have sent supplies to South Carolina when they were needed in Virginia. Others said his government wasn't strong enough to fight the war. They said Jefferson was not an effective leader.

And in his heart he knew it was true. He had always trusted his beliefs, but now—too late—he realized that his ideas weren't right for the situation. He had believed that a strong government was the enemy of the people, but during a war (he now knew) the government had to be strong or the country would lose. His friends told him to take a rest. Maybe soon he would change his mind and agree to run again.

No. Never again would he work in government. He was not suited for it. He would retire.

CHAPTER FOURTEEN

War Comes to Monticello

But Thomas Jefferson's problems still weren't over. Early one Monday morning in June 1781, as Thomas was dressing, he saw a soldier he knew riding up to Monticello on his horse. The man rushed in and announced that British soldiers were heading for Monticello!

Thomas gathered his family and fled his own home. The one safe place he could think of was the house of a friend who lived deep in the mountains. Martha packed a few household things and hurried their two daughters into a wagon. Thomas left a couple of loyal slaves behind to try to take care of things. He knew the British wouldn't hurt them: it was the famous Mr. Jefferson they were after.

As the Jeffersons' wagon pulled away, the slaves hurried around the house gathering the silver to hide it from the British. A slave named Caesar got the idea to conceal it under the floorboards of the porch. He pulled them up and jumped down into the hole. Another slave, a young man named Martin Hemings, was handing all the silver down to him when a line of big, burly English soldiers on horseback burst through the thicket.

Moving with lightning speed, Martin threw the last of the silver down to Caesar, slammed the floorboards in place and stood on them. A big British officer, Captain McCleod, rode up to him.

"Where's the governor?" he demanded.

Martin stood still, looking straight ahead and hoping that Caesar wouldn't make a sound.

"Which way did he go?" Captain McCleod asked angrily.

Still Martin didn't move or speak.

A soldier jumped down off his horse and ran up to him. He grabbed Martin by the collar and stuck his pistol into his chest. "If you don't tell us which way Governor Jefferson went," he hissed, "I'll blow your heart out."

Martin started to tremble. Then he suddenly looked into the soldier's eyes and smiled. "Fire away then!" he cried.

The soldier looked up at his captain. Captain McCleod shook his head. "Listen here," he said. "If you tell us where the governor's silver is, we'll let you live."

"Yes sir," said Martin. "It was all sent up to the mountains. That's all I know."

The soldier grabbed him again. "Let me kill him, Captain," he snarled.

Captain McCleod stared hard at Martin for several seconds. Then he shook his head. "Let him go."

The British troops stayed at Monticello for two days. They slaughtered the cows and pigs, killed the horses, burned the barns and all of Thomas's carefully tended corn, beans, peas, and tobacco crops. Captain McCleod admired the magnificent house too much to destroy it.

The slaves breathed a sight of relief when the soldiers finally left. Happiest of all was Caesar, who had spent two days in the dark hole under the floorboards!

When the Jeffersons returned home, they were greeted by the heartbreaking sight of destruction and burnt, smoldering fields. This was too much to bear. As Thomas approached the house, tears welled up in his eyes.

In a moment, the slaves were clustered around him talking excitedly. When he had heard the story of their loyalty, he did break out in tears, but they were tears of gratitude.

Even now, Thomas Jefferson's troubles weren't over.

Martha had been ill off and on during the past few years. The flight from the British had weakened her further. In the spring of 1782, she suddenly turned worse and was forced to stay in bed. Thomas tried to help take care of her, but his sister was the one who looked after her while Thomas walked in and out of her room, asking again and again if she needed anything.

She remained sick all summer. Thomas watched over her constantly, always hoping for signs of improvement. Then, one September day, she turned worse. Thomas panicked. He held Martha in his arms and talked to her. He told her he was sorry for causing her so much pain. It was his fault that they had been forced to run from the British.

He would make things better in the future, he said. He would stay at home from now on, and they would raise their family together at Monticello. He told her about new trees and vines that he was planning to get from Italy. He said soon Monticello would look as lovely as it used to. He even promised to practice the violin until he was as good as she was on the harpsichord. They could play together as they use to.

Martha didn't speak and didn't open her eyes, but Thomas felt her hand grip his arm. Tears came into his eyes. His sister called the servants, who led him out of the room. Outside the door, his ten-year-old daughter Patsy stared at him with wide, frightened eyes. He hugged her.

A few minutes later, his sister came out, her head bent low. Martha was dead. For the only time in his life, Thomas Jefferson fainted.

Things Begin to Grow

For a long time after his wife's death, Thomas stayed locked in his room. Servants brought his meals to the door. He barely touched them.

After several weeks he emerged. He began riding his horse. He would ride up and down over the hills around Monticello, his mind a swirl of painful thoughts. He had failed Virginia. Now Martha, whom he had loved more than anything in the world, was gone.

What should he do? Nothing seemed worthwhile anymore. He decided that he would stay right here, in the hills that he loved. He would live the rest of his life at Monticello as a farmer, raising his daughters and tending to his fields.

And for many months that is what he did. He returned to farming, his first love. In his sadness, he had a tremendous desire to make things grow.

The British had destroyed much of his farmland. He now began the difficult task of restoring his wonderful crops. At Monticello he had grown cherries, peaches, oranges, plums, walnuts, spices, beans, cauliflowers, tomatoes, pumpkins, turnips, squashes, carrots, and many other plants. His was the largest selection of crops in Virginia, probably in the whole country. He was proud of his land, and wanted to return it to its old health and beauty, and to continue experimenting with new kinds of fruit and vegetables. Throughout his life he was to import olives, strawberries, figs, and other plants from all over the world. The fields of Monticello were the first in America to grow many of the fruits, vegetables, and spices that we take for granted today.

He always said that farming was the proper work of any man, and that farmers were the best of citizens. "Cultivators of the earth," he wrote, "are the most valuable citizens. They are the most vigorous, the most independent, the most virtuous, and they are tied to their country, and wedded to its liberty and interests by the most lasting bonds." He loved farming because it made a man independent. Now, working on his farm and bringing new life to the scarred land helped to ease his pain.

And slowly, as he dug and sweated and worked alongside the slaves and hired men, he did begin to feel better. The earth felt solid and healthy in his fingers. The rain was cool and refreshing. He set about rebuilding parts of Monticello that had fallen into disrepair during the war. The clanging of hammers and shouts of workmen filled the air. The sun shone down on the rich land and revealed newly blooming vines and shoots. Nature was doing its work: his fields were growing once again.

Thomas liked to work in the fields himself. The slaves would watch in amazement as he dug away at the tough soil. They told each other that they had never heard of a master who worked his own fields.

For hours on end he worked in the hot sun, digging and sweating, and thinking about the past few years. He believed he had failed his country and his family. With shame still lying heavy on his chest he stabbed at the earth and thought about the future. Could he make amends? He would like to, but how? What could he possibly do?

Then one day in the spring of 1783, a letter came. The people of Virginia wanted Thomas Jefferson to become a member of Congress, to serve them in Philadelphia.

He considered it for a long time. He had said before that he would never work in government again—it had made him too depressed. But here, he told himself, was a chance to start again. He might be able to help his country.

The Americans had won their rights now—the war with England was over. General Washington, seven years after his humiliating retreat from New York City, had returned in triumph with his troops, parading through the streets amid cheers. But there was still so much to be done. Now came the job of making laws to insure that the rights Americans had fought for were guaranteed.

Thomas Jefferson smiled. He knew he was making the right decision. He had helped Monticello to begin growing again, now he would help his country to grow. He sat down and wrote a letter accepting the job. He would go to Philadelphia.

Thomas Jefferson spent only six months in Congress. Eager to get back to work helping his young nation, he did many things in that short time that changed America forever.

He helped to decide what the future states of the country would be. At that time, of course, there were only thirteen states, the original colonies. But even then, people knew that someday other lands in the West would want to become states. Thomas helped to draw the boundaries of the new lands. He also thought up names for them.

He thought a great deal about what the names should be. He tried to choose names that were beautiful, and he thought he had done a good job. But when he read his names to the Congress, everyone smiled, then began to laugh. The names were so difficult they thought he must be joking. Thomas Jefferson proposed calling one state Cherronesus, another Assenisipia, and another Metropotamia. One member of Congress teased Thomas that people would never be able to remember those names. Thomas, his face reddening, nodded. He saw what the Congress meant.

However, Congress did like some of his suggestions. They thought Michigania was a pretty good name, but they simplified it to Michigan. And they changed Illinoia to Illinois.

While in Congress, Thomas also proposed to establish a single unit of money in the states, as he had discussed with Ben Franklin seven years before. He suggested they use the Spanish silver dollar. The Congress liked this idea and adopted it, although in the end they just called it the dollar. Thomas Jefferson was also the one who suggested breaking the dollar up into one hundred parts, called cents ("cent" means "one-hundredth").

Thomas also made another try at bringing an end to slavery. The bravery and loyalty his own slaves had shown during the British occupation of Monticello was still in his mind. He now wrote a bill proposing that slavery be forbidden in any new states. Six northern states supported the bill, but the South (including Virginia) opposed it. The bill was defeated.

He still believed in his heart that owning human beings, as if they were property, was morally wrong. "Nothing is more certainly written in the book of fate," he once wrote, "than that these people are to be free." On the other hand, he continued to keep slaves at Monticello. This difference between his feelings and his personal actions was still there.

While in Congress, Thomas even wanted to change the units of weight and measurement—pounds to kilos and feet to meters. Congress said no to this idea, which was too bad, because today we are still trying to change to metric units. If we had done it back then measurements would be much simpler today.

America's foreign affairs were in a confusing state at this time. As a new country, it had to decide how to set up relations with other nations, and which of the European countries it would trade with. America needed diplomats to represent its interests abroad. The Congress had to choose a wise, experienced man to help represent America in France. It chose Thomas Jefferson.

Thomas accepted at once. In this position he would be able to help shape America's foreign policy. It was a particularly important job because the French had helped the Americans during the war. Thomas thought it was crucial to maintain good relations with them.

The time abroad would be good for him, too. Though he had been busy in Congress for the past months, he was often overcome with sadness. He thought about Martha constantly. His failures as governor still weighed on him. Here was a chance to do new things, to help him make up for the past.

All his life, he had immersed himself in European culture: the grand buildings, beautiful paintings, and great thinkers. The Declaration of Independence was full of European ideas, ideas he had gathered from books. At last he would get to visit the places where his most cherished ideas were born.

And he was also happy that he wouldn't be alone in Europe. His daughter Patsy, now almost twelve years old, was coming with him.

On July 5, 1784, in Boston Harbor, Thomas and Patsy Jefferson boarded a big sailing ship named the *Ceres*. As the ship pulled away from the dock, Thomas put his hand on his daughter's shoulder and the two of them watched the land move away. Behind them was Boston

"Washington returned in triumph."

Harbor, the scene of the "tea party" which had inspired the American colonists to rebel.

Father and daughter turned and looked forward. Out there, far ahead, was Europe. He was heading for the Old World, where America's roots lay. He knew it well from books. Now he would finally see it.

CHAPTER SIXTEEN

A New Life in the Old World

P aris was bigger, noisier, dirtier, and more frightening than any city in America. It was also much more exciting. Streets and alleys criss-crossed and zigzagged so that the whole city was like a gigantic puzzle. Around every bend was a new sight, sound, and smell. Old women dressed in rags hud-dled on the corners, selling apples, flowers, bits of cloth. Finely dressed soldiers rode high on their horses down the central streets, eyes straight ahead. Choruses of voices floated out of old stone churches, singing solemn Latin masses. Every street had its own smell: chestnuts, oranges, frying garlic.

Soon after he arrived, Thomas Jefferson found that he was a famous man in France. Even before he and Patsy had settled into their new home, invitations to parties began pouring in. Everywhere he went, people intro-duced themselves. Everyone wanted to say a few words to the famous author of the Declaration of Independence.

Thomas reveled in the attention. In America he was also a respected man, but in Paris everything was done so lavishly, so richly, that it aroused Thomas's sense of

"Paris was busier, nosier, dirtier..."

the excitement and adventure in life. He felt like a new man. Practically every evening he attended magnificent balls where the women wore fantastically colored silk gowns and the men adorned themselves with rings, velvet coats, and lace ruffles. And these lords and ladies of the French nobility formed circles around Thomas Jefferson. To them he was an exciting rebel from the rough and ready land of America. They exhausted him with questions.

Thomas and Patsy had some American friends to help them adjust during this time of dizzying excitement. Two other men had been appointed with Thomas Jefferson to represent America in Paris, and they were none other than John Adams and Benjamin Franklin. Adams and his wife, Abigail, and daughter, Nabby, helped the

Jeffersons to get used to life in the European capital. Nabby took Patsy to dressmakers' shops and helped her to choose a wardrobe in the fancy French style.

But Thomas hardly needed help. He took to the elegant life-style almost immediately, while John Adams, though he had been in Europe for several years, had never been able to get used to Parisian finery. Being from New England, where simple, direct manners and styles were considered the best, he always felt uncomfortable amid the gaiety of French high society.

Ben Franklin held the official position of American ambassador to France. Thomas was extremely pleased that his old friend and adviser was in the city. Although Franklin was old and often in pain, he liked to attend parties when he could. His ready wit made him enormously popular with the French. Thomas enjoyed many evenings of quiet conversation at Franklin's elegant house on the outskirts of the city.

It wasn't long before Franklin had to give up his post and return home; he was just too ill to continue serving his country. It was no surprise that Thomas Jefferson was chosen to replace him as the official ambassador. Although Thomas was sorry to see his old friend go, he was pleased at being granted the post. It meant that he would have a chance to help make the ties between America and France strong. It also meant that he would be spending at least several years in Paris, which he had quickly grown to love.

During those years, Thomas entered wholeheartedly the vibrant, colorful world of Parisian society. He attended parties where he charmed the hosts with his broad knowledge of science and European affairs. The ladies were especially taken with the tall, gallant man from the rugged land of America. Their pretty eyes flashed at him across ballrooms. At first, Thomas ignored their glances. Later, softening to European ways, he began smiling back.

Thomas became a regular figure at the city's salons, where philosophers, writers, and scientists gathered to discuss the great events of the time: scientific experiments that were taking place all over Europe; new ways to calculate distances; ships that sailed faster and safer. One man, a natural scientist named Buffon, infuriated Thomas by telling him his theory that animals in America were always smaller than in Europe. Thomas spent a great deal of money to have bones, teeth, and skins of American deer, elk, beaver, and moose shipped to France. He then proudly displayed them for Buffon, and it was all he could to to keep from bursting into laughter when the Frenchman was forced to admit he was wrong: these specimens were much larger than anything in Europe.

Thomas also got a chance to travel through Europe and take in the sights of France, Italy, Germany, and the Netherlands. These were not just pleasure trips, though. He was always alert for ways to improve life in America, especially farm life.

He heard of a variety of rice grown in Italy that he thought would do well in the American South and determined to send some home. But when he got to Italy, he found that it was against the local law to export rice from the region—and the penalty was death! Thomas made up his mind to send some of this rice to America. He hired a man to smuggle a bag of the rice out of Italy on his mule. Just in case the man got caught, Thomas filled his own pockets with rice and rode back across the border, half afraid the Italian authorities would stop him and ask to look in his pockets!

Thomas also had high hopes that many other crops could be grown in America. He sent dozens of Italian olive trees to South Carolina and Georgia, hoping that the farmers there would begin olive farming (it never caught on). He also inspected vineyards in France and Germany and had grape growing operations set up in Virginia. Of course, he always had Monticello in mind when he thought of agriculture. Whenever he sent rice, olives, grapes, and other crops to America, he made sure that some went to his own farm.

Back in Paris, Thomas met with his European friends and told them excitedly about his plans for developing America's farms. "Such a strange man!" they thought. How could one man be so interested in government and science—and farming too? Still, they found his broad range of interests fascinating. He was an all-around thinker who fit perfectly in their intellectual society. The French loved Thomas Jefferson, and Thomas loved France.

In England it was a different story. The French people revered the man who had helped defeat their old rival,

England. But the English had a very different opinion of him!

Nevertheless, in the fall of 1787, Thomas made a trip to England. John Adams was now the American ambassador to the court of King George. Adams had invited his friend to come to London to meet their old enemy face to face. Now that America was a nation in its own right, Adams hoped to try to improve relations between the two former enemies.

An ornately decorated coach picked up the two American statesmen and drove them through the streets of London to the palace. As they approached, Thomas's mouth fell open in wonder. St. James Palace was set in an enormous park, beautifully laid out. They rode down a magnificent tree-lined avenue through a forested area where deer and squirrels watched them pass. Stately buildings appeared through the trees.

As he walked through the grand entrance of the palace, Thomas couldn't help but compare its stately dignity with the extravagant styles he had seen in France. The wide halls and solid arches and columns made it seem as though the palace would stand for all time.

They were shown into the royal reception hall. Bishops, government ministers, and ambassadors from other countries stood talking in groups in the richly decorated room. After the two "colonials" had waited for what seemed like hours, the steward, a dignified old gentleman, announced the king.

King George entered the room, huffing and looking red in the face. He glanced around at the faces in the room,

"King George entered the room."

then looked at the steward with a scowl. The steward presented Thomas and John Adams to the king one at a time.

"Mr. John Adams, ambassador from the government of America," he announced first. John Adams, who was used to the formalities of the palace, bowed low and addressed the king politely. King George nodded.

"Mr. Thomas Jefferson, ambassador from the government of America to the court of King Louis of France," said the steward.

Thomas bowed low.

Everyone in the room looked on in shock as the king of England turned his back on Thomas Jefferson and walked away! John Adams looked at his friend in surprise, then at the king. He didn't know what to do.

Soon some of the other guests approached them and began talking. Everyone pretended that nothing had happened, but they all knew very well what had happened: the king had refused to speak to Thomas Jefferson, the author of the Declaration of Independence. After all, Thomas was the one who had written to all the world that King George was "unfit to be the ruler of a free people." King George, it seemed, had no intention of greeting this man.

Thomas, though, had always believed in politeness. He had been taught always to be decent to people, even if they had been your enemies. "The British," he wrote to a friend after his visit to St. James Palace, "require to be kicked into common good manners."

In 1789, after five years in France, Thomas Jefferson was called back to America. Although he had fallen in love with France, he had recently been longing to return home, to see family and old friends, and most of all to return to Monticello. But suddenly, just as the letter from Congress reached him, things began to get particularly exciting in Paris. The French Revolution began.

Thomas had sensed that the Revolution would come. There was a great gulf between the rich aristocracy—knights, earls, dukes, and so on—and the poor peasants. Thomas had observed the conditions of the many peasants and had written to friends back home:

Of twenty million people supposed to be in France,
I am of the opinion there are nineteen million more

wretched, more accursed in every circumstance of human existence, than the most conspicuously wretched individual in the whole United States.

Eventually, these people got fed up with their rulers. They began to declare that it didn't make sense for a man to rule the country just because his father had. One Frenchman, named Beaumarchais, wrote a play called *The Marriage of Figaro*. In it, a barber talks to a prince. He says:

Because you are a great lord, you think you are a great genius! Nobility, fortune, rank, place: all that makes you so proud! What have you done to deserve all these blessings? You took the trouble to be born, and nothing more. Otherwise, you are a rather ordinary man.

This is what many of the French people were thinking at the time. And on July 14, 1789, they showed King Louis of France what they thought of him. On that day a huge crowd of people formed in the streets of Paris and stormed the Bastille, the great stone prison where the King kept his enemies. Thomas watched in amazement as the crowd, getting wilder and more violent ran through the streets breaking windows, raiding shops, drinking, and singing.

Thomas stayed long enough to see this violence erupting in the streets. And as he watched he thought how different it all was from the American Revolution. The Americans had revolted because their rulers were unjust and they wanted to set up a free, democratic government in which the people would have the power.

In France, however, the people knew they wanted to get rid of their leaders, but they didn't all believe in democracy. There were many different classes of people in France—churchmen, peasants, aristocrats—and each class had different opinions about how the country should be run.

Thomas was fascinated by these differences between the revolutions in America and France. He wondered how the French Revolution would turn out.

He could not stay to see for himself. After five years in Europe, Thomas and Patsy Jefferson left for home. Back when they were on board the boat coming to Europe, they had both felt nervous about entering the strange world of France. But in five years Patsy had grown from a twelve-year-old girl to a seventeen-year-old young woman. They had gotten so used to France that it seemed almost like home. As their ship left the harbor, they told each other a secret: now they were both nervous about returning to America!

CHAPTER SEVENTEEN

The New Mood at Home

No sooner had the ship pulled into Norfolk Harbor in Virginia than Thomas and Patsy began to notice how different everything was. Clothes, buildings—everything had changed in five years! It all looked so rough and simple to the two of them. What had happened?

Actually, America hadn't changed all that much. Thomas had changed. He had gotten used to the more refined and graceful life of Europe. He had forgotten that America was a rough, young country of wilderness and simple towns.

But some things really had changed: people's ideas. Thomas wrote to a friend that Americans were "no more like the same people; their notions, their habits and manners . . . so totally changed."

It was now 1790, fourteen years since Thomas had written America's Declaration of Independence. When he wrote it, people were stirred by the idea of being free from the king's rule. All of their thoughts came down to one word: freedom. But in the past several years they had realized that freedom wasn't enough. A country needed a strong government if it was to survive. So while Thomas was away their ideas and habits had changed.

The country was now called the United States of America. Before, it had been America. While Thomas was in Europe the people had decided that the government was too weak. In 1787, delegates from all the states met in Philadelphia to write a Constitution to strengthen the government. This meeting was called the Constitutional Convention. Now under the new constitution, instead of the states being separate in most things, they would be united. They would act together through the Congress and through the new leader, the president.

When Thomas left for France there was no such thing as a president. At that time, the states felt that if one man were put in charge of the entire country he would become a tyrant, a harsh and unjust ruler. In the past several years most Americans had realized that the country needed a strong leader.

In spite of his experience as governor of Virginia, Thomas still preferred a weak government to a strong one. He was not completely happy that America had grown to favor a strong government. Even he had to agree, however, that it was necessary to have a president.

It was obvious who the first president should be: General George Washington, the most famous and most popular man in America. He had been a military leader for 35 years. Already he was looked upon by ordinary Americans as a legend.

When Thomas first heard about the new Constitution, he worried about how strong the president could become. When he learned that Washington had been elected as the first president he relaxed—General Washington had always used power wisely.

President Washington asked Thomas Jefferson to be his secretary of state. Thomas accepted, but he was secretly disappointed because he had been hoping to go back to France. So instead, he brought some of France to America. He filled his new house in Philadelphia with French furniture, which he had shipped over himself. And when he gave dinners for his friends in the government, he served fine French food and French wines.

While his friends didn't have much experience with Europe, they liked Thomas's new way of life, especially the food and wine. His best friend now was James Madison, a wiry little man who was so short that when he stood talking to Thomas, his head only came up to Thomas's shoulders. Madison was many years younger than Thomas and respected him tremendously. He was always asking Thomas for advice, and even copied his dress and manners. Like Thomas, he was naturally shy and not a particularly good speaker. But when friends were gathered for dinner he relaxed and became quite lively, jumping around in his seat and telling stories.

James Monroe was another good friend. Monroe was the soldier who Thomas had sent from Richmond to watch the British troops. He was a serious young man with sharp eyes and tight lips. He believed in the rights of citizens very passionately. He talked so intently that everyone around couldn't help but listen. He always sat straight-backed at the table and moved his head in quick, bird-like jerks when he looked around, his sharp eyes taking everything in.

Thomas worked closely with Madison and Monroe while he was secretary of state. All three men believed that the government's main job was to protect the rights of individual citizens. They were concerned that some people in power were making the government too strong.

There was one man in Washington's cabinet whom they all agreed was dangerous: Alexander Hamilton, the secretary of the treasury. When Thomas and his friends gathered, Hamilton was their favorite subject. Hamilton, they believed, cared more about his own power than about the rights of citizens.

One evening, Jefferson, Madison, Monroe, and another friend, William Small, were talking over dinner. They sat at Thomas's long oak table, each with a wine glass in front of him. Madison was saying that they should never trust Hamilton, because he had once said America should be ruled by a king.

"I don't know if that's true," James Monroe said.

"It's true!" Madison cried. He then told them a story which they had all heard a hundred times. It was about something Hamilton had done a few years ago during the Constitutional Convention.

"One day," James Madison began, "I was sitting in the front of the room and Hamilton rose in the back. He said that America shouldn't be a democracy at all, but should follow the English system. He thought America needed a really strong leader—a king!"

Hamilton's love for power made Thomas Jefferson

and his associates wary of him. In their caution they overlooked the fact that it was Hamilton who had first realized that the new nation needed a firmer structure. Before he was even thirty years old, this lively, quick-witted young man was busy writing articles which argued in favor of a Constitution that would define which powers resided with the federal government and which resided with the states. Without Alexander Hamilton's work, the Constitution might never have come to be.

It wasn't just Hamilton who worried Jefferson and his friends. Washington's vice president was none other than John Adams, Thomas's old friend. Adams had also come to support a strong federal government.

Back in 1776, when they had first met, Thomas Jefferson and John Adams had agreed on the one important matter: that America must break away from England. Now that the break was final, they had very different opinions of what would make the best kind of government for the new nation. Adams preferred a powerful leader. He thought the title "President" didn't sound very important. He said he would rather the country had a king who would be elected by the people. This idea frightened Jefferson, Madison, and Monroe.

Often during these days, dinner conversation turned to what would happen after Washington's term was finished. James Madison said it was obvious who the next president should be: Thomas Jefferson. Monroe and Small immediately chimed in: "Here, here!"

Thomas surprised them by saying he wasn't interested in being president. He was tired of fighting Hamilton. He had already told Washington he wanted to return to Monticello.

James Monroe raised his eyebrows. James Madison flew out of his seat and grabbed his friend by the shoulders.

"Why, we won't let you do such a thing!" he cried. "You are needed in government. You must run for president!"

Thomas was firm. He would retire at the end of the year.

"But what will you do at Monticello?" James Monroe wondered. "You are too young to retire. You will get bored!"

Thomas said there were other important things in life besides running a government. There was science and farming, and there was his family. He missed his daughters very much.

Madison sat back down. Eventually the conversation changed to other topics. The others talked about science, then France, then wine, but Madison was quiet. Thomas saw that Madison was staring off into space, deep in thought, busy thinking up one of his great plans.

At the end of that year, 1793, Thomas gave up his position as secretary of state and returned to Monticello. It was a pleasure for him to spend time with his daughters again. By now Patsy was married. She and her husband and their two children all lived at Monticello and the house was alive with the cries and laughter of children.

It was a long time since Thomas had lived at Monticello. Plenty of work needed doing. The crops had not been rotated properly and the fields were scarred by erosion. While the house had been completed, Thomas was eager to tear part of it down and rebuild. His mind was still full of images of the magnificent houses of Europe. He had seen so many artful and impressive buildings that at one point he had wanted to leave Europe immediately just to get home to Monticello and begin building all over again. In France, he had taken careful notes of all the designs he liked. He now had a whole new plan for Monticello outlined.

With boyish eagerness, Thomas set about rebuilding. Soon the place was alive with the clanging of hammers and the shouts of builders. Thomas had a brick factory built which was shortly producing bricks by the ton. "We are now living in a brick kiln," Thomas wrote to a friend. He also set up a nail factory which turned out ten thousand nails a day.

Meanwhile, back in Philadelphia, James Madison was a very busy man. He knew that Washington was not going to run for a third term. He had also learned that John Adams was determined to become the second president.

Adams, Hamilton, and others who believed in a strong federal government had been given a name. They were called the Federalists, and their party was called the Federalist party. Jefferson, Madison and those who believed that citizens and their local governments should have the power—and that a strong Federal government was dangerous—were called Anti-Federalists, or Republicans.

The two parties opposed each other even more than Democrats and Republicans do today. The system of government was still very young and, as with a baby, it needed time to grow and become strong. Each party feared the policies of the other might kill the country. Men and women felt that the next election was critical to the direction of American democracy.

Thus, James Madison had a big question on his mind: If Adams was going to be the Federalist candidate for president, who would be the Republican candidate?

As far as Madison was concerned, there was only one man in America who was popular enough to win: Thomas Jefferson. But Jefferson would not run. Madison did a great deal of thinking. Finally, he came up with a plan. He would campaign for Jefferson for president without Jefferson knowing about it!

Thomas Jefferson was probably the only presidential candidate in our history who spent his entire campaign building a house. By the time he found out what was going on, the election was so close that he couldn't stop the campaign. He was in the running.

At that time the law said that whoever got the most votes would be president, and the second-place man would be vice president. Thomas remembered all too clearly how he had not been strong enough as governor of Virginia. He was worried now. He secretly hoped he would come in second.

He did. It was a close election, with 71 electoral votes

for Adams and 68 for Jefferson. Thomas got what he wanted—the vice presidency—but now he was in a tough position. He and Adams were no longer very friendly to one another—in fact, they almost never spoke. They represented opposing political points of view. Now they had to run the government together!

On inauguration day, Thomas decided it would be best to arrive in Philadelphia quietly, by public coach, so Adams, the new president, would get all the attention. Besides, he thought, nobody would be too interested in the vice president.

He did not realize that there were many people in the country who still believed in the principles of the revolution. These men and women agreed with Jefferson that the best government was one that would not interfere in the lives of citizens. Jefferson had always put his faith in the decency of ordinary people, not in institutions. Many people understood this. Thomas Jefferson, author of the Declaration of Independence, was their hero. He was the one man who truly understood the rights they had fought for. They were determined to show how they felt about him.

Just outside Philadelphia the coach had to stop. The road was completely jammed with people. There was so much noise that Jefferson and the other passengers got out to see what the commotion was.

People clogged the road, and a company of soldiers stood at attention. Across the street was a banner saying "JEFFERSON, THE FRIEND OF THE PEOPLE." The soldiers saluted him. The cannons fired sixteen rounds. Everyone cheered.

Thomas blushed crimson. It was such a shock! And despite the fact that he had hoped to steal into the city quietly, this mass greeting warmed him. Sometimes he felt that he was the only one in the country who still believed in the principles of the revolution. To see so many people showing their support for him, and for the ideals of individual liberty, made him happy and relieved. Americans had not lost their dreams.

CHAPTER EIGHTEEN

The Thinker
Takes Charge

While Adams was getting used to his duties as president, and Thomas Jefferson was presiding over the Senate (one duty of the vice president), something strange was happening out at sea. French pirates were busy raiding American ships! France was now at war with England, and America had been doing business with England. The French thought they'd get back at England by hurting the American trade.

In towns all across America, people read of the French raids with growing anger. Some said America should cut all its ties with France. Some began to blame the vice president. After all, they figured, Thomas Jefferson had lived in France for five years. He had many French friends. He was a well-known admirer of France and French ways.

In Philadelphia, Thomas heard their complaints calmly. He answered that, despite the current problems, it was wisest for America to keep its ties with France. President Adams, who was also furious at the French, felt that strong action was called for. However, he listened

126

to Thomas's advice and sent two men to France to try to patch up the differences. The men returned with scandalous news. The French official they had met with refused to speak to them unless they gave him a bribe of $250,000!

The scandal made newspaper headlines across America. Soon people were standing on street corners in cities and towns, talking excitedly about how horribly France had treated the United States. Many called for war. President Adams and several members of the government agreed. War with France was the only answer.

Soon shipyards clanged with activity. Government offices in small towns were jammed with men who wanted to enlist in the army. Adams gave speeches about bringing the French nation to its knees. Congress passed laws forcing French residents in America to leave.

Thomas Jefferson stood by through all of this, always calm. Reason, he had always believed, was the most powerful tool in the world. He tried to reason with people, to show them that they were acting recklessly.

Despite his efforts, many Republicans in the government changed parties and became Federalists. They agreed with Adams that France must not be allowed to get away with its humiliating treatment of America and her representatives. As French nationals were forced to leave the United States, Thomas apologized to his French friends in Philadelphia and watched with regret and shame as they boarded ships for France.

In the end, America did not go to war with France.

Tempers cooled and slowly things began to return to normal.

Thomas Jefferson did not return to normal. He had watched as people let themselves be caught up in war fever, and he didn't like what he had seen. The Federalists in the government, he decided, had acted dangerously, inflaming passions and sparking the desire for revenge in the American people.

He made a decision. He would run for president in the next election. He would run against John Adams and the Federalists, and this time he would win.

The election campaign of 1800 was a vicious one. Federalists and Anti-Federalists accused and threatened one another in a frenzy of hatred.

Newspapers controlled by the Federalists portrayed Jefferson as a weakling. They published cartoons of him as governor of Virginia, running away from the British. Since Thomas Jefferson was against a strong government, they said, he must be against the Constitution—against the United States itself. One paper went so far as to say that if Jefferson were elected president, "murder . . . will be openly taught and practiced, the air will be rent with the cries of distress, and the soil will be soaked with blood, and the nation black with crimes."

But there were also many Republican newspapers, and here the picture was very different. The Republicans wrote that Jefferson was "the man of the people," who believed in rights and not in war. Aware of Adams's earlier wish for America to be governed by a king instead of a president, the Republican newspapers printed cartoons of Adams dressed in long robes with a crown on his head.

Many people were ashamed of how they had become carried away in calling for war with France. They remembered that Thomas Jefferson had stood firm through the panic and argued sensibly against the war. They knew him as a calm, intelligent man, as a champion of the rights of ordinary people.

They turned out and voted for him. On February 16, 1801, Thomas Jefferson became the nation's third president.

On a clear, cool afternoon in March, Thomas Jefferson rode with his friends down a wide dirt road, chatting nervously. He was about to become the first president to be inaugurated in the nation's new capital, Washington, D.C. Just ahead was the Capitol Building. It wasn't finished yet. Scaffolds and ladders stood around its bare walls. One man said it looked like "two wings without a body."

Thomas rode proud and erect, thrilled and awed by the responsibility he was about to take on. He was dressed in simple, drab clothes. His days as an elegant dresser trying to impress his bride-to-be were long over. He now preferred a simpler style.

Once inside the Capitol, Thomas became even more nervous. He had to give his inauguration speech before a huge crowd of all the important men in the government. He sat near the podium, waiting to be sworn in, his long

The Capitol Building wasn't finished.

legs clacking together in fright. His voice never carried well, and he was afraid that no one would even be able to hear him.

When it was time for him to speak, he tried his hardest to make his voice boom out like Patrick Henry's used to, but it just didn't work. Only the first few rows of people actually heard his speech—which was too bad, because this was one of the greatest inaugural speeches ever given.

He had many friends in the audience, and many enemies. He made them all comfortable by saying, near the beginning: "We are all Republicans—we are all Federalists." He went on to talk about his favorite subject, rights. The purpose of a government, he said, was to ensure the rights of its citizens to live as they saw fit. That was why he was a Republican.

"I know that some honest men fear that a Republican government cannot be strong, that this government is not strong enough," President Jefferson said. "I believe this is, on the contrary, the strongest government on earth." He argued that it was the strongest because it was "a wise and frugal government, which shall restrain men from injuring one another, which shall leave them otherwise free to regulate their own pursuits of industry and improvement."

This was the author of the Declaration of Independence talking. In the Declaration, Thomas had stated that America wanted a government that would ensure the rights of all people, including "life, liberty, and the pursuit of happiness." Now, he said, America had such a government. There were problems with the system, but it was working. And as he spoke he felt a tremendous satisfaction, because he knew that he had helped make it work.

The people of the country knew it too. They cheered him in the streets of Washington, D.C.—and in Boston, New York, Pittsburgh, Baltimore, Richmond, and most other places.

People everywhere felt they knew him. He was nearly sixty years old now. He had written the Declaration twenty-five years earlier. Parents made their children memorize parts of it. They told them stories about what it was like to be alive when America was fighting her great war for independence.

They told about the great fighter of the revolution, George Washington, and about the great speaker, Patrick Henry, and about Thomas Jefferson, the great writer and thinker of the revolution.

He had written the Declaration when he was thirty-three years old. He had changed since then. He was still in good health, though sometimes he had pains in his legs and had to bandage them. He was a grandfather now. His red hair had all turned white, but he still stood straight and tall. His eyes were still clear and pierced whatever they looked at like arrows.

As he got older, he had grown more carefree and informal. As a young lawyer he had been shy, and had dressed and behaved with great formality. Now he kept a little gray and white mockingbird in his study at the "President's House," as the White House was then called.

One day when an important official was reading a report, the dignitary was amazed to see the bird fly right on top of the president's head. Seeing the official's expression, Jefferson began to laugh. He told the man to stop reading. He said he wanted to show him something really important. He then proceeded to demonstrate how the bird could sit on his arm and eat bread crumbs right out of his lips.

Many people were comfortable with President Jefferson's informal ways—but not everyone. The first time Thomas met the British ambassador, Anthony Merry, the ambassador was shocked at how poorly dressed the president of the United States was. He wrote to the king that Jefferson wore "pantaloons, coat, and underclothes indicative of utter slovenliness and indifference to appearances."

Mr. Merry, a very proper man, never really trusted Jefferson after that, and the worst was yet to come.

Once, Mr. Merry and his wife were invited to a dinner party held at the President's House. According to formal courtesy, the President was supposed to honor the guests by walking with Mrs. Merry into the dining room. Thomas forgot, however, and walked in with Dolley Madison, James Madison's lively and talkative wife.

Mr. and Mrs. Merry were horrified. They were used to the strict formalities of European courts. Mr. Merry wrote to the king, saying he and his wife felt they had been insulted by the president's behavior.

When Thomas's friends explained to him what he had done, he decided he'd better apologize. He tried to make amends by sending Mrs. Merry a packet of flower seeds. To his mind seeds were a wonderful gift—a present that would grow into something alive and beautiful—but Mrs. Merry didn't see it at all. Why in the world would anyone send her seeds? She couldn't understand. She decided the president was making a joke of some kind. So even Thomas's apology backfired.

Thomas Jefferson wasn't the only one to have changed in the years since the revolution. The country itself was very different from that summer in 1776 when Thomas Jefferson had written its birth certificate. There were thirteen states then. Three new states had been added: Vermont in 1791; Kentucky in 1792; and Tennessee in 1796. And most of the land up to the Mississippi River was now part of the country as well.

Thomas Jefferson was not content to stop there. He knew there was land beyond, thousands of miles of wild, beautiful, untamed land, and he was determined that while he was president he would make it part of the United States.

Much of that land was owned by France and Spain. He was no soldier, and he hated war. While he wanted those lands very badly, he would not go to war over them. Instead, he thought a great deal about how he might convince the European powers to give them up, and he waited.

But by the end of his first year as president it looked as if war might come anyway. Spain closed the port of New Orleans, so that American ships could no longer use it. Americans were indignant. Many felt the United States had a right to claim the city, and they began to call for war. Even many members of Congress told the president that, this time, war was inevitable. Spain was blocking America's trade in the West. They should fight back and take the lands around the Mississippi River.

Thomas sat in his office and shook his head. He was levelheaded by nature and it amazed him how excited people got over such incidents. Couldn't they see that Spain was a powerful country? Didn't they realize that New Orleans wasn't important to America right now? Thomas gave a firm "no" to the plans for war. He had learned to be strong.

134

The crisis passed. People began saying again that Jefferson was right to wait calmly. They looked up to him for handling the crisis intelligently.

Thomas had not forgotten about the Western territories. During the next year Spain sold Louisiana to France. Thomas sent his secretary of state, James Madison, to talk the matter over with the representatives of Napoleon, France's leader.

President Jefferson got lucky beyond his wildest dreams. Napoleon decided to give up his lands in America in order to concentrate his attention on France's conquests in Europe. He offered to sell the whole area to the United States.

This time, Thomas didn't ask anyone's advice on what to do. He accepted the offer and bought the land. This became known as the Louisiana Purchase. It was a remarkable purchase because at that time Louisiana didn't mean just the state, but the entire area from the Mississippi River to the Rocky Mountains—the vast middle of the continent.

It cost the U.S. fifteen million dollars—a very reasonable amount, for with one stroke of his pen on that day in 1803 Thomas Jefferson almost doubled the size of the country! It became one of the largest peaceful land acquisitions in history. Because Thomas was intelligent enough to wait for the right time, he was able to avoid war and simply buy the land.

One day not long after he had signed the Louisiana Purchase, Thomas sat in his bedroom gazing out the window at the forests that surrounded Washington. Adding

"It cost the U.S. fifteen million dollars."

so much land to the country made him prouder than almost anything else he had ever done. He had made it possible for America to grow.

He was about to send a team, Lewis and Clark, off to explore the West. It would be such an adventure! He thought of his childhood: how he had dreamed of becoming an explorer like his father! For a moment he wished that he could go with the exploration team into that vast unknown.

It would never be, though. He was an old man. He sighed. The adventure of exploring and settling the American West would be left for future generations.

Thomas Jefferson Still Survives

One evening in March 1809, Thomas Jefferson attended a ball at the President's House. It had been years since he had danced, but tonight he had a good reason to celebrate. His closest friend, James Madison, had just become the fourth president of the United States.

Thomas Jefferson had served two terms as president. Friends had urged him to run for a third term, but he told them he agreed with George Washington that eight years was enough for any man. He was weary of politics and looked forward to returning to Monticello.

He greeted Madison at the entrance to the ballroom. The new president looked pale and nervous. Mrs. Margaret Bayard Smith, the wife of a newspaper editor, hurried up to Mr. Jefferson's side.

"Mr. Jefferson," she whispered, "why is it that you are so cheerful, while President Madison looks so worried? After all, it's his party."

Thomas chuckled. "I have got this burden off my shoulders," he explained, "while James has now got it on his."

137

An hour or so later, Mrs. Smith came up to Thomas again. Smiling coquettishly, she pointed out that all the ladies at the ball had been following him around the room.

"They would have to," Thomas said with a smile, "since I am too old to follow them."

Within a few days Thomas boarded a carriage and headed home to Virginia. He was retired now, but he did not feel old. He was happier than he had been for a long time. All his life, he had loved to think and plan. Now he was free to spend his time on the projects he loved. Maybe he was too old to go exploring in the West, but that wasn't going to stop him from exploring other things.

Monticello wasn't exactly a quiet retirement home. By now it was famous not only as the home of the renowned Thomas Jefferson, but as one of the finest buildings in America. Visitors came daily to see the house and estate. There was the great clock, designed by Jefferson, which used cannonballs from the Revolutionary War as weights. Hung over the doorway were antlers of strange wild animals brought back by Lewis and Clark from their exploration of the West.

Visitors were fascinated by the way Jefferson had hidden the kitchens and stables beneath the yard on both sides of the house. Although the house was basically complete, Thomas was never quite satisfied. Every month or two he would think of a new feature or improvement and there were always new innovations to read about and try out.

Thomas now had a flock of grandchildren around him. Whenever he was feeling old, they were there to make him young again.

In the afternoons he would often take a break from writing letters to walk out on the lawn and watch the children running races and playing games. In the evenings he would sit before the fire and read. He liked it when they read too. One of his granddaughters wrote:

> When the candles were brought, all was quiet immediately, for he took up his book to read and generally we followed his example and took a book—and I have seen him raise his eyes from his own book and look around on the little circle of readers, and smile.

His favorite books, as in his student days, were in Latin and Greek. He had an enormous library to choose from, one of the biggest in America. In 1815, realizing that Congress needed a library, he sold his books to the government. This was the start of the Library of Congress, which is today the world's largest library.

During his retirement, Thomas's greatest interest was in the minds of the future citizens of America. He believed that the American government would only continue if the American people were educated enough to understand the importance of their freedom. "Knowledge is power, knowledge is safety, knowledge is happiness," he once wrote. America needed schools if it was to be strong, safe, and happy.

He designed a plan for something brand new—a sys-

"He liked it when his grandchildren read too."

tem of state education. His idea was that education should be available to all children, not just those whose families could pay for it. He wanted Virginia to set up a school system. He also began work on a state university.

The University of Virginia was the state's university. But everyone knew that it was really Thomas Jefferson's. After all, he got the state government to approve the plan. He organized people to help build it. He surveyed the grounds himself, using the skills his father had taught him over seventy years before. He decided what subjects would be studied and who the teachers would be.

And, of course, he designed the buildings. He didn't want it to be just one big building, but an "academical village" in which the students and professors would live and study together. It would be an ideal university, beautiful and efficient, made of separate buildings around a big courtyard, with a covered walkway connecting them all.

It took him eight years to organize the plans for the university. By the time he finished he was eighty-two years old. As usual, there were people who didn't like one thing or another about his plan. But he knew this would be his last great project and was determined to make it work. He was pleased with the final form of the university and wrote: "Our university is the last of my mortal cares, and the last service I can render my country."

Every mail delivery brought dozens of letters to the famous old father of the Republic, many of them from people he didn't know. One day Thomas was surprised to find one envelope with curiously familiar handwriting. He stared at it, lost in thought, but he couldn't think whose it might be. He opened it.

It was from John Adams in Massachusetts. The two men hadn't seen or spoken to one another since Jefferson's election as president. They hadn't been friends since they were both in Europe, and that was twenty-five years ago. They had become enemies because of politics and they had remained enemies. But now, after all these years, Adams had taken the first step toward friendship.

"You and I ought not to die before we have explained ourselves to each other," he wrote.

Thomas agreed. He wrote back.

In the last years of their lives the two great men exchanged over one hundred letters and became the best of friends once more. They wondered whether they would ever see each other again. For a time they thought they might. They were both invited to a special celebration in Washington. It was 1826, and in July the nation was going to celebrate its fiftieth birthday. The leaders in Washington invited the two men who had helped to create the nation to the big celebration.

But at Monticello Thomas Jefferson, who had been ill, suddenly turned worse. He developed a high fever. He knew that he would never make it to Washington. He couldn't move from his bed and his grandson, Thomas Randolph, took care of him. The young man looked nervous and worried, but his grandfather told him to relax, that what was happening was natural.

"I am like an old watch," Thomas Jefferson said, "with a pinion worn out here and a wheel there, until it can go no longer."

He would sleep for hours, then wake up and ask if young Thomas would like to hear a story. He told him about the events leading up to the Revolution: how Patrick Henry's voice had resounded through the House of Burgesses in Williamsburg when he first heard him speak, how the news of the Boston Tea Party had thrilled the Assembly. He told his grandson about Ben Franklin and the story of the hatmaker. He even remembered tiny details, like what the temperature was on July 4, 1776.

He became worse and could no longer speak. He tried to hold out. He wanted to live until the fiftieth anniversary of the Revolution. On the night of July 3, he suddenly opened his eyes and looked around. His daughter Patsy was sitting beside his bed.

"This is the fourth of July?" he asked hopefully, his tired face stretched with pain.

"Just a few more hours," she whispered.

He didn't speak again, but he made it. Thomas Jefferson died just after noon on July 4, 1826. He was 83 years old.

Meanwhile, four hundred miles away in Massachusetts, John Adams lay dying, too. Incredibly, both men died on the same day, exactly fifty years after their legendary decision on independence.

John Adams's last words were: "Thomas Jefferson still survives!"

He didn't know that Jefferson had just died. But, in a way, John Adams was right. Thomas Jefferson helped his dream of democracy to take root in America. The idea caught on, just as he thought it would. In time, it spread to dozens of lands in Africa, South America, and Asia where people declared their independence, fought revolutions, and proclaimed democratic governments. Thomas Jefferson's ideals were not only American; they survive today in deserts and jungles, on mountains and plains all over the world.

In this country, although Jefferson was never able to put an end to slavery in his time, the idea of freedom that he had believed in survived and grew with the years. In his will, he freed some of the Monticello slaves. Some of these free black men and women, knowing that Virginia was still no place where they could be treated fairly, moved west.

They went to the new territories—to Ohio, Wisconsin, and further west—hoping for a good life in the newly settled lands and waiting for the day when they, too, could take part in the freedoms that Thomas Jefferson had helped bring to America.

Adams, Abigail
Wife of John Adams.

Adams, John
Second president of the United States. Friend and supporter of Thomas Jefferson at the Second Continental Congress.

Anti-Federalists
Also called Republicans. This party was led by Thomas Jefferson, and was opposed to a strong central government for the United States.

Architecture
The art and science of building.

Bastille
The name of an infamous prison in Paris, France. It was stormed by the people at the start of the French Revolution on July 14, 1789, and later demolished completely.

Battle of Lexington
A skirmish in Lexington, Massachusetts, which took place on April 19, 1775, between colonial farmers and British soldiers. It was the first battle of the American Revolution.

Battle of Trenton
Took place on December 26, 1776, in Trenton, New Jersey. After a dangerous crossing of the icy Delaware River, the colonial army, led by George Washington,

surprised and defeated the British soldiers. It was the first big victory for the Americans.

Boston Tea Party

In December of 1773, citizens of Boston disguised as Indians secretly boarded British ships and dumped shipments of tea overboard as a protest against taxes.

Carr, Dabney

Friend and brother-in-law of Thomas Jefferson.

"Common Sense"

Pamphlet written by Thomas Paine to urge Americans to declare their independence from Great Britain.

Constitutional Convention

The meeting of representatives from the thirteen states in 1787 at Independence Hall in Philadelphia to draft and adopt the United States Constitution.

Continental Congress

The first meeting of representatives from all thirteen colonies at Carpenter's Hall in Philadelphia. They discussed problems they were having with British rule.

Cornwallis, General Charles

British general during American Revolutionary War.

Currency

Money in circulation—whether in the form of coins or paper notes. Thomas Jefferson organized and streamlined the currency system in America.

Declaration of Independence

Document written by Thomas Jefferson in which the colonists declared themselves independent from the rule of England, and set down briefly the principles upon which the new country of America was to be founded.

Federalists
Party led by Alexander Hamilton which believed that the American states must support a strong central government.

Franklin, Benjamin
Leading American statesmen, scientist, printer, philosopher, inventor, and diplomat.

Gage, Thomas
British general during the Revolutionary War.

Hamilton, Alexander
Secretary of the treasury under George Washington. A brilliant economist who did much to organize the Federal government. One of the founders of the Federalist party.

Hancock, John
The president of the Second Continental Congress, which adopted the Declaration of Independence.

Harrison, Benjamin
Patriot leader, delegate to Congress from Virginia.

Henry, Patrick
Patriotic leader from Virginia, who was known as an inspirational speaker. He is remembered for a great speech in which he said, "Give me liberty or give me death!"

Hessians
German soldiers who were paid to fight for the British. These paid soldiers are called "mercenaries."

147

House of Burgesses
Assembly in the colony of Virginia which resembled the English Parliament.

Inauguration
The ceremony by which the president of the United States of America is officially sworn into office.

Jay, John
Delegate to the Continental Congress from New York. Later, he was chief justice of the Supreme Court.

Jefferson, Jane
Older sister of Thomas Jefferson.

Jefferson, Jane Randolph
Thomas Jefferson's mother

Jefferson, Martha
Thomas Jefferson's wife.

Jefferson, Martha (referred to in book by her nickname, Patsy)
Thomas Jefferson's older daughter.

Jefferson, Peter
Thomas Jefferson's father.

King George III
The British king during the time of the American Revolution.

Lee, Richard Henry
Delegate to Congress from Virginia. He introduced resolutions on June 7, 1776, seeking independence from England.

Lewis and Clark
Explorers sent by Thomas Jefferson to explore the territory of the Louisiana Purchase.

Library of Congress

Thomas Jefferson sold his library of 6,000 volumes to the U.S. Congress to begin the Library of Congress. A previous collection owned by Congress was destroyed in the War of 1812.

Little Mountain

The place where Thomas Jefferson built his famous home, Monticello (which means "little mountain" in Italian).

Locke, John

18th century English philosopher who wrote about new ideas of government and whose ideas had a great influence on Thomas Jefferson.

Louisiana Purchase

In 1803, Thomas Jefferson arranged for the United States government to buy a huge piece of land from the French government for fifteen million dollars. This land, called the Louisiana Purchase, stretched from the Mississippi River to the Rocky Mountains.

Madison, Dolley

Wife of James Madison.

Madison, James

Friend of Thomas Jefferson. He became fourth president of the United States of America.

Monroe, James

Friend of Thomas Jefferson. He became fifth president of the United States of America.

Monticello

Thomas Jefferson's house which he designed and built.

Newton, Sir Isaac

18th century English mathematician and physicist. His work revolutionized physics, and his ideas had a major impact on thinkers of the day, and also on Thomas Jefferson.

No-cake

A kind of corn cake eaten in Virginia in the 1700's.

Paine, Thomas

American author and political philosopher. Author of "Common Sense," a pamphlet which inspired many American colonists to throw their support behind the idea of a revolution.

Pantops

A mountaintop near Shadwell, Thomas Jefferson's father's plantation.

Plantation

A large farm usually worked by slave labor, producing a major cash crop. The economy of the south was almost entirely dependent on plantations in Thomas Jefferson's time.

Randolph, Peyton

Virginia delegate to the Continental Congress, replaced by Thomas Jefferson.

Secretary of State

The person in the president's cabinet who is in charge of foreign affairs. Thomas Jefferson served as secretary of state under George Washington.

Shadwell

The plantation of Jefferson's family.

Slavery

The practice of owning and using human beings for work. Slaves could be bought and sold like property and were not protected by the Constitution. The economy and way of life in the south were dependent on slavery.

Small, William

Thomas Jefferson's college professor who introduced him to new progressive political ideas which were called "The Enlightenment." These ideals greatly influenced Jefferson's later political activities, in particular his writing of the Declaration of Independence.

Stamp Act

British Act taxing all written material (including letters and newspapers) in the American colonies. This tax was very unpopular.

"Summary View of the Rights of British Americans"

Paper written by Thomas Jefferson for the Virginia delegation to the first Continental Congress. It was then published by friends, and started his fame as a writer.

Tomahawks

A kind of short-handled hatchet used as a weapon by North American Indians.

Washington, George

Leader of the American army during the Revolutionary War and the first president of the United States of America.

1. Why was Monticello a special house? What does it tell you about Thomas Jefferson?
2. Describe what you feel was the most important thing Thomas Jefferson did. Why?
3. What did Thomas Jefferson leave behind that we remember today?
4. Who was Thomas Paine? How did he contribute to the cause of the American colonists?
5. From your reading, write a page on Benjamin Franklin. What was his contribution to America?
6. What was the Boston Tea Party? Why did the citizens of Boston disguise themselves as Indians?
7. Thomas Jefferson and George Washington were very different men and very different leaders. What contribution did each man make to the formation of the United States of America?
8. What would Thomas Jefferson think of the United States today, in your opinion? Would he be surprised at how the nation has turned out?
9. Who was Alexander Hamilton? Why did he and Thomas Jefferson disagree with each other about America's future?
10. Research the differences between the Federalists and the Republicans. How were their ideas of America different?
11. The colonists who participated in the Boston Tea

Party were breaking the law. Do you think they were justified in what they did? Why?

12. Research the Stamp Act of 1765. Why were the American colonists so opposed to this Act? What did they mean by "No Taxation Without Representation?" Choose a side—British or American—and argue that point of view on this issue.

13. Do you think England could have avoided the war with the colonies? If you were King George III what would you have done? Do you think he could have done anything?

14. Thomas Jefferson believed that reason was the most powerful tool in the world. What is reason? Do you think Thomas Jefferson was right?

15. Benjamin Franklin told Thomas Jefferson that founding a country was like being a scientist in a lab working on an experiment. How successful would you say was the "experiment" performed by the Americans of 1776?

16. Thomas Jefferson wrote, "Knowledge is power, knowledge is safety, knowledge is happiness." What did he mean by this? Do you agree or disagree?

17. Patrick Henry said in a famous speech on the eve of the American Revolution, "Give me Liberty or give me Death!" Do you agree with this statement?

18. In the Declaration of Independence, Thomas Jefferson wrote:

"We hold these truths to be self-evident, that all men are created equal, that they are endowed by their

Creator with certain unalienable Rights, that among these are Life, Liberty and the pursuit of Happiness."

Explain what you think Thomas Jefferson meant by these words.

19. Imagine you have to establish the government of a brand new country. What kind of government would you create?

20. In the Declaration of Independence Thomas Jefferson wrote that ". . . all men are created equal." Yet in 1776 a substantial part of the population were slaves. The slaves would not gain their freedom until the Emancipation Proclamation of 1863. What does this say about America in 1776? Does it make you feel differently about the Declaration of Independence?

21. The Americans won the Revolutionary War even though they were a smaller country than Great Britain (in terms of population), had a less well-trained army, and less money. Why do you think the colonists won?

Andrist, Ralph K. "To the Pacific with Lewis and Clark." *American Heritage, The Magazine of History, 1967.*

Bliven, Bruce. *The American Revolution.* Random House, 1958.

Colby, Jean Poindexter. *Lexington and Concord, 1775: What Really Happened.* Hastings House, 1975.

Commager, Henry Steele. *The Great Declaration: A Book for Young Americans.* Bobbs-Merrill, 1958.

Davis, Burke. *Black Heroes of the American Revolution.* Harcourt Brace Jovanovich, 1976.

Glubok, Shirley. *Home and Child Life in Colonial Days.* Macmillan, 1969.

Ketchum, Richard M., Editor. *The American Heritage Book of the Revolution.* American Heritage, 1971.

Leckie, Robert. *The World Turned Upside Down: The Story of the American Revolution.* Putnam, 1972.

Lomask, Milton. *The First American Revolution.* Farrar, Straus & Giroux, 1974.

Munves, James. *Thomas Jefferson and the Declaration of Independence: The Writing and Editing of the Document that Marked the Birth of the United States of America.* Scribner's, 1978.

Nolan, Jeanette Covert. *The Shot Heard Round the World: The Story of Lextington and Concord.* Messner, 1963.

Phelan, Mary Kay. *The Story of the Boston Massacre.* Crowell, 1976.

Snyder, Gerald S. *In the Footsteps of Lewis and Clark.* National Geographic Society Special Publications Division, 1970.

Wright, Louis B. *Everyday Life in Colonial America.* Putnam, 1966.

The Expansion of the United States After the Revolution

Here is an activity which will help you to understand the expansion of the United States. On the following two pages there is a map of the United States as it appears today, except for Alaska and Hawaii. Color in red the original thirteen states. Remember that Maine was a part of Massachusetts, West Virginia was still a part of Virginia, and Vermont was claimed by New York at the time of the Revolution. Color these three states in pink. Next, color in green the states which came from the territory of the Louisiana Purchase of 1803. This territory stretched from the Mississippi River to the Rocky Mountains. Include Colorado and Wyoming. Color in blue the states east of the Mississippi and west of the original thirteen states. This land belonged to the United States in 1803. Color in orange the state added from Spain in 1819. Color in purple the states which were once a part of Mexico. Now color the remaining area in yellow. This was called the Northwest Territory and was under British control as of 1845.

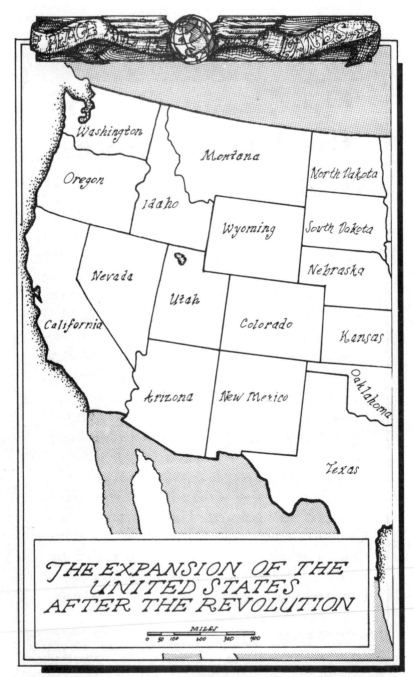

THE EXPANSION OF THE
UNITED STATES
AFTER THE REVOLUTION

MILES
0 50 100   200   300   400